THE BOOK OF
ROSS-ON-WYE

FRONT COVER: A peaceful scene on the horseshoe bend.

Under Helle (a secret place) was on the Gloucester Road side of the Market
Place until its demolition in the last century.

THE BOOK OF ROSS-ON-WYE

A STUDY OF AN ANCIENT TOWN

BY

MARTIN H. MORRIS

BARRACUDA BOOKS LIMITED
BUCKINGHAM, ENGLAND
MCMLXXX

PUBLISHED BY BARRACUDA BOOKS LIMITED

BUCKINGHAM, ENGLAND

AND PRINTED BY

FRANK ROOK LIMITED

TOWER BRIDGE ROAD

LONDON SE1

BOUND BY

BOOKBINDERS OF LONDON LIMITED

LONDON N5

JACKET PRINTED BY

CHENEY & SONS LIMITED

BANBURY, OXON

LITHOGRAPHY BY

SOUTH MIDLANDS LITHOPLATES LIMITED

LUTON, ENGLAND

DISPLAY SET IN BASKERVILLE

& TEXT SET IN 12/14PT BASKERVILLE

BY BRIAN ROBINSON

NORTH MARSTON, ENGLAND

© Martin Morris 1980

ISBN 0 86023 083 X

Contents

Acknowledgements

This book could not have been compiled without the help willingly given by many public bodies and individuals. They include the Assistant Registrar of the Royal Archives at Windsor Castle; the Keeper of the Public Records Office, London; Robin Hill, Reference Librarian at Hereford, and the staff of the County Library at Ross and Hereford; Miss S. Hubbard, Assistant County Archivist; Ross Town Council; Leslie Price and other members of the staff of the South Herefordshire Agricultural Co-operative Society Ltd; the Midland Bank at Ross; D. Grigg, W.D. Massey, J.G. Hillaby, R. Okell, Mrs K. Turner, C.J. Metcalfe, C. Grant Dixon, Mrs E.C.M. Richardson, R.G. Hicks, Nigel Heins, Mrs P. Tonge, Mrs E. Morris, R.G. Williams, R.P. Morgan and Miss M. Morris.

Many photographs have been received from the *Ross Gazette,* Walbrook Photography, G.L. Ward, J.M. Hall, J.K. Gabb, J.C. Coombes, Miss Anne Sandford, Curator of Hereford Museum, and I am also indebted to Mrs I. Davies for permission to reproduce several photographs taken by her husband, the late R.E.P. Davies, in the early years of this century. Valuable assistance with illustrations has also been given by Mrs A. Butcher and her family, John Ashby, Basil Butcher, J.M. Tommey, John Trivett, the *Hereford Times,* Milwards, G.G.Gwatkin, Mrs H.W. Ruston, M.J.A. Winch, Mrs E. Passey, T.W. Passey, Group Captain Hugh Lynch-Blosse, (Secretary of the Wyedean Tourist Board), Mrs Dorothy Powell, Mrs F.F. Beckett, B.C. Hackett, OBE, J. Tugwell, E.J.Rowberry, I. Woolf, P. Llewellyn, Miss H. Smith, Mrs N.I. Forbes-Guy, Mr and Mrs A.W. Davies, Trevor Collier, C.E. Parsons, E.R. Arnold, Ian Ashpole, R.H. Shaw Batchford, R.H. Roff, G.Bullock, F.J. Handley, F.J. Parsons, Rev Paul Wheatley, the *Ross-on-Wye Advertiser,* Craig Horle of the Religious Society of Friends, R. Nicholas Stephens, E.J. Rawlins, Woodville Polymer Engineering and the Haigh Engineering Company. To all I am most grateful.

Dedication

To my Daughters.

Foreword

Martin Morris arrived in Ross at the age of eight. At the end of his first term at school the class was asked to draw a map of Ross. Martin set to work with enthusiasm and came out top. This love and enthusiasm for Ross has stayed with him all his life. I think Ross-on-Wye captures the hearts of all who come to live here, no less than those who were born in this lovely part of England. Martin has worked on the *Ross Gazette* for over 30 years now, and there is nothing he doesn't know about us or our town, and his special interest has been the history of the town. Indeed, in 1973 he wrote what I believe is the only book entirely devoted to its history: *Reflections of Ross-on-Wye*. Now he has written what I am sure will be The Book of Ross-on-Wye for many, many years to come.

With its enchanting illustrations, its succinct writing and its dry humour, this book will fascinate all who live in Ross-on-Wye or its beautiful environs, as well as delight and inform the many thousands of tourists who visit us each year. Ours is a town of some antiquity, as the reader will learn, and the book sketches its history from the early Roman settlement at Ariconium nearby, through its growth first as village and then as market town, with all the traumas it had to face during the Civil War. Different chapters neatly describe the growth of its churches, its institutions, its industries and its sports.

When you have enjoyed reading it, it will find its natural place in your guest room.

Margaret Shepherd

The Man of Ross

But all your praises why should Lords engross?
Rise, honest Muse, and sing the Man of Ross.
Pleas'd Vaga echoes through her winding bounds,
And rapid Severn hoarse applause resounds.
Who hung with woods yon mountain's sultry brow,
From the dry rock who bade the water flow,
Not to the skies in useless columns tost,
Or in prowd falls magnificently lost.
But clear and artless pouring through the plain
Health to the sick and solace to the swain.
Whose causeway parts the vale in shady rows,
Whose seats the weary traveller repose
Who taught that heav'n directed spire to rise?
'The Man of Ross' each lisping babe replies.

Behold the market place, with poor o'erspread,
The Man of Ross divides the weekly bread.
He feeds yon almshouse, neat, but void of state,
Where age and want sit smiling at the gate.
Him portion'd maids, apprentic'd orphans bless,
The young who labour, and the old who rest.
Is any sick? the Man of Ross relieves,
Prescribes, attends, the med'cine makes and gives.
Is there a variance? enter but his door,
Balk'd are the courts and contest is no more.
Desparing quacks with curses fled the place,
And vile attornies, now a useless race.

Lord Bathurst —   Thrice happy man enabled to pursue
What all so wish, but want the pow'r to do.
Oh say, what sums that generous hand supply,
What mines to swell that boundless charity?

Pope —   Of debts and taxes, wife and children clear,
This man possess'd - five hundred pounds a year.
Blush, grandeur, blush! prowd courts withdraw your blaze,
Ye little stars, hide your diminished rays.

Lord Bathurst —   And what? No monument, inscription, stone,
His race, his form, his name, almost unknown.

Pope —   Who builds a church to God and not to fame
Will never mark the marble to his name,
Go, search it there, where to be born and die,
Of rich and poor, makes all the history.
Enough, that virtue fill'd the space between;
Prov'd by the ends of being to have been.

Alexander Pope

Living History

On a damp, chilly afternoon, six days before Christmas in 1934, I came to Ross-on Wye. There had not been room for me in the furniture van that carried my father and elder brothers, and my mother and I had come by 'bus from the mining town in the Forest of Dean where I was born. Clutching her hand, I walked along Gloucester Road. And suddenly I saw the Market House. To a boy of eight it was huge and awe-inspiring. Looking back over nearly half a century, I realise the Market House was symbolic of the vast differences between my native town, which was a product of the Industrial Revolution, and this ancient borough with a history going back 1,000 years. Ross was exciting. Round nearly every corner was enchantment — a black and white house, a Tudor almshouse, a fortress-like tower, the imposing facade of the Walter Scott School. The towns are not ten miles apart, but they are as different as the shaded, magical woodland of the forest is from the open pastures cradling the River Wye.

Sunday brought more soul stirring. As a family we had always attended Evensong. I had been christened in a church which was not 50 years old, had plastered walls and the minimum of ornamentation. Now I was in an edifice rich with the skills of craftsmen over six centuries and filled with the memorials to those who had served their generation. Spellbinding was the upright figure of the Cavalier, Colonel Rudhall, with his stone eyes gazing into the infinities of time and space.

My working life has been largely spent as a newspaper reporter, recording the news of this town of 6,270 people (1971 Census) surrounded by a rural area of 11,000. Now news can no longer be news once it has been served to the reader and digested. It would be the most perishable of all commodities, save that it dissolves into indestructible history.

What has gone can never be changed — but alas, it can be forgotten and versions of it can be distorted. In probing the history of this town, I have had several long-held beliefs shattered. There are tales that I should have enjoyed recounting, but have refrained from doing so because after all these years I have found them to have little substance. The stories of King Edmund Ironside's death in Ross and King George IV's unexpected arrival I have retained as matters of interest, though the former is probably legendary and details of the latter cannot be authenticated as fully as I would wish.

Only with a certain amount of surmise can the story of this fascinating town be completed, and I hope the difference between this and undisputed fact is made clear in the chapters I am about to unfold.

In Rosse sunt. vii. hide geld. In dnio. e una car' 7 alia
posset. ee. Ibi. xviii. uilli 7 vi. bord' 7 pbr cu. xxiii. car'.
Ibi. iii. serui 7 molin de. vi. solid 7 viii. den' 7 xvi. ac pa.
Silua. e in defensu regis. Uilli redd't. xviii. sot de censu.
In Upton sunt. vii. hide geld. In dnio sunt. ii. car' 7 xviii.
uilli 7 xi. bord 7 ii. buri 7 pbr. Int' oms hnt. xx viii. car' 7 dim'.
Ibi. v. serui 7 iiii. ac pa. 7 una haia. 7 Silua nichil reddes.

LEFT: The entry for Ross in the facsimile edition of the Domesday Book
(Public Record Office E 15/97). RIGHT: Ross on a map of Herefordshire in
1577. BELOW: This part of Cleeve Land has not significantly changed since
it was part of Offa's Dyke, more than 1,000 years ago.

12

Rule of the Bishops

Where the tree-covered foothills of the Forest of Dean plateau merge into the pastures of the River Wye, Ross was born. Its recorded history stretches back not quite 1,000 years, yet men were living in the neighbourhood in the Ice Age 60,000 years ago. The Marches of Wales were at the limit of the glaciated region of the Pleistocene epoch and man found shelter in a cave on the limestone Doward Hill, which looms above the river as it pierces the Yat Gorge on its course from Herefordshire to Gwent. The cave had its inhabitants in the succeeding Stone Age, Bronze Age, Iron Age, and when the Roman legions came.

Three miles east of Ross, at Weston-under-Penyard, the Romans built the iron-manufacturing town of Ariconium, and maybe they trod the land now covered by the shops and streets of Ross, for they lie in direct line with Ariconium and the fordable stretch of the Wye at Wilton. The armies were certainly four miles down the river at Bishopswood, for there they abandoned a treasure which remained hidden until 1895, when three earthenware jars, crammed with 18,000 coins, were found nine inches beneath the surface of a hillside. The coins, of the Constantine period (290-360AD), were from many parts of the scattered Empire — Constantinople and Croatia, Antioch and Carthage, Thessalonica and Rome itself.

Ancient man, maybe the warrior Silures, lived on Chase Hill, the magnificent backdrop to Ross. On its summit is the site of a camp covering 20 acres, with solid rock cut through to a depth of at least 12 feet.

Offa's Dyke was at the foot of the hill. The Wye is regarded by some as the old frontier decreed by the Mercian king in the eighth century, but members of the Woolhope Club who climbed the Chase in 1901 decided that the dyke came from the river meadows, along Cleeve Lane, past the Firs to The Vine Tree Inn and then along the line of the road to Walford. Curiously, the route was marked by holly bushes.

The intersection of Cleeve Lane with the road to Hom Green was named Baker's Oak, probably because a tree was planted there to mark the town boundary.

Ross was a village in Saxon times and an almost forgotten legend suggests that it was where Edmund Ironside, King of the English, died by an assassin's hand in 1016. Master Walter Map, a man of letters from Herefordshire and a clerk in the household of Henry II, told the story in his *de Nugus Curialium* (Courtiers Trifles). The 1924 translation by Tupper and Bladen Ogle relates how when the kingdom was divided between Canute and Edmund, a slave of Ironside thought that if he could contrive his master's death and make Canute master of the entire kingdom, his reward would be great. When Edmund came to his villa at Minsterworth in Gloucestershire, the slave put in the opening of the latrine a long, sharp spit.

The story goes on, 'The slave walked before him with the light of many candles and he turned some of them so that Edmund unawares fell upon the spit and was pierced with a deadly wound. He had himself borne to Ross, the King's village which he had granted to Hereford Church, and which it still possessed, and there he died'.

The slave happily went to Canute but his only reward was to be hanged from the highest oak.

Walter Map must be regarded as a romanticist, but, if nothing else, the tale has the worth of showing that 800 years ago Ross was of sufficient consequence to be a topic at the Plantaganets' court.

The earliest undisputed documentary evidence of Ross is in Domesday Book, 1086 and transcribed, reads — 'In Ross are seven hides paying geld. On the demesne is one plough and there could be another. (There are) there 18 villeins and six bordars and a priest with 23 ploughs. (There are) there three serfs and a mill worth six shillings and eight pence and 16 acres of meadow. The wood is in the King's forest. The villeins pay eighteen shillings as revenue.'

Mention of a priest gives proof that Ross had a Saxon church and 'the wood is in the King's forest' points to hunting requiring the King's licence and being subject to Forest Law. Harold, Earl of Hereford and for a few months King of England, had taken from the bishopric the woods of Ross. These were restored by Roger, Earl of Hereford, in the reign of Henry II.

Ross was no ordinary manor, but an Honour containing many manors and fees. Conflict over the boundaries was inevitable and on 28 January, 1227/28 a commission proceeded to the King's forest of Penyard and set out by metes and bounds the division between the King's fee of Penyard and the Bishop's fee of Ross.

The Bishop's fee extended from the Chase to the Bishops's brook (which rises near Ruardean), and James Wood, MA, LLB, in a paper to the Woolhope Club in 1902 made the interesting surmise that the town of Ross took its name from, and did not give its name to, the district. The uplands of the Chase and Bishopswood exactly represented the Welsh 'Rhws' as contrasted to the lowland to the westward.

It is generally held that the 'Rhws' is the tongue of upland upon which the church and centre of the town now stands, but if Ross did have its beginnings at the Brookend, as Fosbroke and others have claimed, there would be no logical reason other than Mr Wood's theory for it being given a name derived from a promontory.

Over a mile away, at the foot of the southern slope of the tongue, was another settlement, described in Domesday as; 'The King holds Clive (Cleve, a tithing in Ross). Earl Harold held it. (There are) 14½ hides with a berewick called Wiltone (Wilton). On the demesne are 4 ploughs and (there are) 20 villeins and a reeve and 11 bordars with 16 ploughs. (There are) there 9 serfs and 5 bondwomen and one oxman. (There are) there 2 mills worth 6 shillings and a fishery which renders nothing. To this manor belong so many Welshmen as have eight ploughs and render 10½ sestiers of honey and 6 shillings and 5 pence'.

This suggests that Clive was more substantial that the village of Ross and further supports the theory that the entire area was known as 'Ross'.

Clive and its berewick of Wilton straddled the river at its ford, so the town of Ross may owe its origins not to the ford but to the service it gave the countryside with its mill. This service was developed by it becoming a market town when about May, 1138, King Stephen granted to the Bishop of Hereford, Robert de Bethune, a Thursday market in Ross. Possibly this was some reward for the Bishop siding with Stephen in the civil war against Matilda, for at this time, on Whit Sunday, 1138, after the fall of Hereford's castle, Stephen is said to have attended a Mass of Thanksgiving in the Cathedral.

King Stephen's grant is known only through its confirmation in 1355 by Edward III. A translation of the undated charter, ascribed by the editors of *Regesta Regum Anglo-Normannorum 1066-1154* to circa May 1138, is: 'Stephen, King of England, to his justices and barons and sheriffs and all his ministers, French and English, of Herefordshire, greetings. Know that I grant to Robert, Bishop of Hereford, to have a market on Thursday each week in his manor of Ross, and I ordain that all men going there and coming back have my firm peace. In witness, Brian, son of the Earl, and John the Marshall, at Hereford'.

On 26 January, 1241, Henry III confirmed this market and granted a three-day fair to Ross on St Margaret's Day (20 July) its eve and its morrow. It was probably Henry who gave Ross the status of borough, which resulted in the manor becoming divided into two, Ross covering the inner part or borough, and Ross Foreign, the remainder of the parish and much of the parish of Walford. Usually, the two manors had the same lord.

In the reign of Edward I, Ross, with other Herefordshire market towns, received writs requiring them to send representatives to the Parliament summoned to meet on 16 February, 1305. Adam de la More and Thomas le Mercer made the long, wearying and hazardous journey to London, but Ross, along with Bromyard and Ledbury, did not appreciate the privilege, and before the summoning of the next Parliament successfully petitioned to be relieved of it on the grounds that they were unable to pay their Members their dues of two shillings a day.

Through the Middle Ages, the Bishops, with their considerable retinue, would frequently visit Ross, staying at their palace between the west end of the church and the north end of the Prospect. 'Palace' would today be regarded as an extravagant description of this unprepossessing building, which was mostly of timber but had a large gateway and porter's lodge, and wings fronting north and west. By the 16th century it was largely in ruins, but for years afterwards the site was known as Bishop's Court, and a small building with a dungeon survived until the 18th century.

The dungeon was for offending priests, and the Cathedral Registers show that John de Aderne bound himself to Bishop Thomas Cantilupe, 1275-82, that 'I will hold him and his successors fully indemnified to the King of England with regards the escape of Ralph and Nicholas, priests, whom for sometime I had in my custody in the Bishop's manor and prison of Ross and who escaped through my negligence'.

Possibly this led to the construction of a more secure prison, for when excavations were made for the building of the Royal Hotel in 1837, a vaulted chamber was found constructed in the rock at a depth of seven feet. Its walls were 5ft 9ins thick, its interior measured 16ft by 12ft, and its only entrance was an aperture in the roof. On each side was a stone bench and there were six massive iron rings intended to receive the prisoner's chain, one ring with the lead attached weighing 72 pounds.

The palace was where the Bishop received his homage and dues, but it was also the scene of jollification. Bishop Richard Swinfield, Lord of the Manor when the building of the parish church started in 1284, liked his worldly pleasures and had a household of 40: squires and pages, serving men, cook, butler, falconer, farrier, and an armed champion to fight for his rights.

He came to Ross in 1286 with a train of 36 horses and showed much hospitality, but there was trouble with the King's Foresters when the Bishop's huntsman coursed in the Chase of Penyard and caught a young stag. To settle the argument of whether the King's rights had been violated, an inquest was held at Howle Hill and this decided that the stag was caught outside the forest in the Bishop's chase.

Swinfield's successor, Bishop Adam de Orleton, did not have such a happy time at Ross. In 1324, he wrote in the Cathedral register: 'When lately I went to Ross to hold a Visitation, a certain son of Belial, William de Irby, Prior of St Guthlac's, canonically ex-communicated, burst into the church with evil intent when I was celebrating Mass on St George's Day and after profane and idle talk, sharpening his tongue like a sword, blasphemously reviled me, though clad in my pontifical vestments and with the clergy and people standing by violently assailed me. Then in spite of my warnings, he stirred up sedition, raised an outcry and assaulted me, disturbing the service and my Visitation to the grave injury of the peaceful King of Kings, in derogation of divine love and in contempt of God's house and to the grave scandal of Christians. I therefore bound him by sentence of greater excommunication'.

In 1334, Thomas Dreylowe, John Saldesowe, Roger Stephens and John Coke were ordered to go naked, save for their shirts and breeches, thrice round the churches of Walford, Ross, and Goodrich, and be publicly whipped before the procession, for threshing the sequestrator's corn 'in contempt of God and the Bishop, to the prejudice of Walford Church, and to the injury of the Church's liberties'.

An indication of the prolificacy of the Bishop's estates is to be found in the misdoings of Walter Moton, warden of the woods. In 1354 he was attached to reply to the Bishop's plaint that he carried away trees to the value of £40 at Ross; entered the Bishop's chase and carried off 500 stags and hinds, 500 fallow deer and 300 roe deer; cut down oak, ash, beech, hazel, whitethorn and elm; broke into the Bishop's free warren at Ross, Upton and Eastnor, and took 500 hares, 1,000 rabbits, 1,000 partridges and 200 pheasants, and took fish valued at £20, including pike, trout, roach, perch, dace and eels. Damages were assessed and he submitted to the Bishop on all points. He also (not surprisingly) resigned the office of warden.

The Bishops also used their holy office to relieve themselves of temporal duties. Bishop Edmund Lacey in 1418 granted 40 days' indulgence to all who should repair the highway from Ross to Wilton.

In 1461, Bishop John Stanbury granted Thomas Martyn and Walter Sewy a lease of the floodgates of the Millpond of Ross, together with the entire take of eels for 96 years, on payment of 3s 4d a year and their undertaking to keep the floodgates and stank in repair.

More than five centuries of the Bishops' suzerainty ended in 1559 when Elizabeth I took possession of the manors under a statute made on her accession that when a bishopric became vacant, the Crown could take over manor land, recompensing the new bishop with tithes and vicarages. Needless to say, the Crown had by far the better of the bargain.

In 1588, Elizabeth granted the manor of Ross Foreign to Edmund Downing and Henry Best. They assigned their interest to the Queen's favourite, Robert, Earl of Essex, and in 1595 all the Crown lands in Ross and Walford were, in consideration of Essex's services, granted on his request to Gelly Meyrick and Henry Lindley. But soon the young earl was to fall from the royal favour, and with his execution and attainder in 1601 and with Meyrick suffering the same fate, the manor of Ross Foreign was granted to Thomas Crompton and that of Ross Borough to Sir Henry Lindley.

On Elizabeth's death in 1603, Essex's widow, who was also the widow of Sir Philip Sidney, bought both manors for £7,000 and they subsequently passed to her son, the third Earl of Essex. On his death in 1646, the manors passed to his sister, Lady Frances Devereux, Marchioness of Hertford, whose husband was restored as second Duke of Somerset with the return of the monarchy in 1660.

It was about 1670 that the Dowager Duchess, as she then was, had the Market House built and granted a portion of the rents of the tolls for 20 years and ten feet of soil round the building for keeping it in repair. Near it stood the Booth Hall where the Court of Pie Powder was held on fair days, the steward of the Manor trying matters in dispute between those coming to the fair. Its name was derived from 'pied poudreaux', (powdered or dusty feet, ie travellers).

On the Dowager Duchess's death in 1674, the manors passed to the fourth Duke of Somerset, but he died only a year later and the manors went to the Dowager Duchess's grand-daughter's husband, the first Viscount Weymouth. They passed through the family, the third Lord Weymouth being elevated to the title of Marquis of Bath in 1789. He died in 1796 and it was his son who put up the manors for auction at Ross in 1818. They were bought for £4,400 by Captain Kingsmill Evans of Hill Court. He too died without issue, and the manors passed to his sister's son, Kingsmill Manley Power. They have since been handed down three times from father to son and are now held by Anselm Manley Power of Hatfield, Hertfordshire. In 1979 the manors have no possessions or authority.

The common seal of the town in the 14th century was a round piece of brass, about the size of a crown piece. The device was a leather water bucket and a sprig of rosemary ('Rose' for Ross and 'Mary' the patron saint of the church) with a Latin inscription, translated as 'The common seal of the town of Rosse. O Christ bless'.

In later years, the town adopted John Kyrle's crest, the hedgehog, and this appeared on the documents of the urban council until 1953 when the council received letters patent granting a coat of arms. The grant is on vellum, the coat of arms being shown at the side. At the head of the grant are the Royal arms flanked by those of the Earl Marshal and the College of Arms. From the foot of the vellum hang the boxed seals of three Kings of Arms.

The Ross coat of arms has a shield divided across into red and green. In the red portion are three leopards' faces reversed with fleurs de lys thrust through, which appear in the diocesan arms and commemorate Ross being the Manor of the Bishops of Hereford. The blue and white wave represents the Wye and the green portion has a fleur de lys from the arms of John Kyrle and an emblem of the Blessed Virgin Mary.

Above the shield is a closed helm surrounded by decorative mantling in green and white. The helm is surmounted by an ancient crown of fleurs de lys, representing the devolution of Ross to the Crown in 1559. From the crown rises a golden eagle, referring to the Roman associations with the district. It wears a green collar and its breast and wings are charged with three red roses, an heraldic pun on the name 'Ross'.

The leafy prospect of Ross from Penyard Hill

18

ABOVE: The enrolment of the confirmation in 1355 by Edward III of King Stephen's grant to the Bishop of Hereford of a Thursday market in Ross. (Public Record Office, Document C66/245). BELOW: The socket of the ancient preaching cross which gave its name to Edde Cross Street. Found at the junction with New Street during excavations c1910, it is now part of the ornamental stonework of the Blake Memorial Gardens.

ABOVE: The Ross coat of arms and BELOW: the 1953 grant of arms.

Kyrle's Profound Influence

The smallest match can light a beacon that will shine in the darkest night. On 22 May in that dreadful year of 1637 when the plague was destroying the lives of many in Ross, a few miles away at the White House, Dymock, there was born one whose profound influence on the town, spiritually and materially, has lasted until the present day.

John Kyrle, The Man of Ross, was not only a liberal benefactor, but his actions in protecting the unversed townsfolk against charlatans and other predators improved the quality of their life, and they and succeeding generations have benefitted from all that he did to enhance the visual and amenity value of the locality.

The Kyrle family originated in Flanders and settled in Herefordshire about the reign of Edward I. In 1295 there was a Robert Curl living at Altone, or Old Town, Court, Ross, and for several generations the family lived at Walford Court. John Kyrle was the son of Walter Kyrle, barrister and justice of the peace, the third husband of Alice, daughter and sole heiress of John Mallet of Berkeley, Gloucestershire. By Walter she had two sons, John being the elder.

He was educated at Gloucester Grammar School and at the age of 17 became a gentleman commoner at Balliol College, Oxford. On his admission, he presented a piece of silver plate to the college, with a promise that when anyone gave a better he would enlarge the gift. This he did in 1670 when he presented what has come to be known as The Man of Ross tankard. It is of massive silver, with a capacity of five pints, and stands ten inches high. The body is supported by little lions and the Kyrle family crest, the hedgehog, arches its back on the thumb-piece.

Kyrle was intended for the Bar but does not appear to have practised, although his legal knowledge was called into service many times after he settled in Ross about the time of the Restoration. His judgement was accepted in individual disputes, sometimes over a friendly tankard, and probably the greatest issue he settled was that in 1674 between the borough and foreign of Ross, concerning the inequality of their taxes, in which he was the umpire between the elected arbitrators.

He was steward of the Lord of the Manor and in 1683 was Sheriff of Herefordshire. He lived in a black and white house in the centre of the town, now known as The Man of Ross House and occupied by the Ross Gazette Ltd and J. F. Hart, chemist.

In person, he was tall, thin, with a plump ruddy face. He usually wore a suit of brown dittos and a King William wig, all in the costume of the day. He never married, but enjoyed good company and exchanging a merry tale. On market and fair days he

21

would entertain nine, eleven, or thirteen, his table including his housekeeper, Judith Bubb, a maiden cousin. Goose was a favourite dish and only on Christmas Day was there roast beef. Malt liquor and cider were the only beverages.

His remarkably good health lasted until a fortnight before his death at the age of 87 on 7 November, 1724. For nine days his body lay in state, people coming from a wide area for the most unusual sight. The room was hung with a black cloth and lighted with wax and at each end of the coffin was a mute. The town's entire population went to the church for his funeral on the evening of 20 November. By his express wish he was buried in the chancel at the feet of his dear friend, Dr Charles Whiting, a former rector.

His only brother being born an idiot, Kyrle left his estate to his kinsman, Vandevort Kyrle. Though unmarried, The Man of Ross was anxious for his name to be perpetuated and decreed by his will that in the event of failure of male issue, the person marrying into the female line should always take and use the name of Kyrle.

He was affectionately known as The Man of Ross in his lifetime, but it was only after his death that his fame became widespread through the writing of Alexander Pope. The poet never knew him personally but gained his information from a Ledbury publisher, Jacob Tonson. In a letter thanking Tonson, Pope wrote, 'My motive in singling out this man was twofold; first to distinguish real and solid worth from showish or plausible expence, and virtue from vanity; and secondly to humble ye pride of greater men by an opposition of one so obscure and so distant from all ye sphere of public glory'.

From Pope's eulogy, published in his *Moral Essays* in 1733, may be traced the benefactions of The Man of Ross. Taking it line by line, it is learnt that Kyrle planted what is today known as the Little Wood on the escarpment facing the river meadows. He gave the town a water supply, by obtaining a long lease on the Prospect, pumping river water to a fountain there containing 550 hogsheads of water, and conveying it by underground pipes to public taps. He restored the causeway linking the town with Wilton Bridge above flood level, and led the appeal for re-building the spire.

As steward of the Lord of the Manor, he collected corn tolls from the market and had them baked in his oven for the distribution of loaves to the poor. Those living in almshouses, the Bluecoat School, apprentices and the sick, were all recipients of his bounty and he drove from the Market Place the quacks and rogues.

Pope, whose lines record an imaginary conversation between himself and Lord Bathurst, showed that Kyrle achieved all this on an income of £500 a year. The stanzas conclude with a rebuke to the population that they had erected no memorial to him. This was rectified c1750 when a blue slate stone was placed within the chancel rails. An elaborate memorial in marble was placed on the north wall of the sanctuary by a bequest of his kinsman, Viscountess Dupplin, in 1776. It has his bust at the top and his motto, 'Virtute et Fide' at the base. On the bicentenary of his death, in 1924, the town at last subscribed a memorial by placing a new clock in the church tower.

Samuel Taylor Coleridge was another poet attracted by Kyrle. When staying in

1795 at The Man of Ross House, by then The Kings Arms public house, Coleridge, wrote:

> Here dwelt the Man of Ross, O traveller hear,
> Departed Merit clames a reverent tear,
> Friend to the friendless, to the sick man health,
> With gen'rous joy he viewed his modest wealth.

But John Wesley seems to have thought the adulation rather overdone. In a letter to the *London Chronicle* on 2 January, 1761, he praised the humanity of the keeper of Newgate prison, Bristol, and asked a little testily, 'Does not the keeper of Newgate deserve to be remembered as well as the man of Ross?'

CENTRE: John Kyrle, The Man of Ross, and LEFT: his memorial in the chancel of the Parish Church. RIGHT: Part of the footpath along the escarpment overlooking the river meadows which The Man of Ross loved, and is still known as John Kyrle's Walk.

LEFT: Kyrle's house as it is
disappeared from Kyrle's house
linotype machine room of the
family arms. CENTRE: On 14
one of the first broadcasts from
story. RIGHT: The house in 1
bust of Charles II on the Mark
loyalty carved on the facing wall
denote either 'Love, 'Loyal' or
trees reputedly planted in the gr
1974, ravaged by Dutch elm d
with

…P: This carved mantelpiece has
…o oak doors are still in use in the
… Kyrle himself punched out the
… 1934, the BBC used the house for
… local personalities told the town's
… RIGHT: Kyrle could not see the
… so he had his own expression of
… heart, a 'C' and an 'L' or 'F' to
… to Charles. BELOW: One of the
… Kyrle fell in the gales of January
… e rest, seen here, were all felled
… eeks.

ABOVE: The chalk bust of Charles put on the Market House at the
Restoration by the local inhabitants, was taken down during repairs in 1955,
and crumbled away. Public subscription paid for a new one made in 1959 by
local sculptor Geoffrey Gwatkin, who became first mayor of recent times
when the office was revived in 1974. *(Hereford Times* photo). BELOW: Alton
Court. This 16th century timber-framed house replaced an earlier Alton (or
Old Town) Court where an ancestor of John Kyrle lived in 1295.

Court Leet to Council

Strides Ross was taking away from its mediaeval setting accelerated at the start of the 19th century. The wooden buildings were fast disappearing and many of the houses and shop premises still to be found in Broad Street, Brookend Street, High Street, Alton Street, New Street, Edde Cross Street and Church Street were already in being.

And now came a dramatic transformation of the contours of the town. Gloucester Road was built across what had been a hollow of some 15-20 feet, to give a gentle incline instead of a steep climb to the Market House. The town's rubbish tip was in the region of the present-day Cantilupe Road and Henry Street.

The roadmakers in this part of the town were building embankments, in contrast to their ancestors who had cut deeply into and through the sandstone rock. The older roads have in places pavements four feet or more above the carriageway, and, notably in Church Street and Alton Street, there are walls of 20ft or so with a solidity more appropriate to a prison than the pleasant secluded gardens at a much higher level than the roadway.

Government of the town rested with the Court Leet and Court Baron, manorial courts that had their origins in Saxon England. A jury at the Court Leet each October selected from three names approved by the Lord of the Manor's steward, who should hold the offices of Mayor (or Sergeant at Mace), four constables, two searchers and sealers of leather, a fish and flesh taster, two market keepers, a hayward, two scavengers and the common crier.

St Margaret's Fair, now known as the Wool Fair, was held in Church Street and other fairs were on the Thursday after 10 March, Ascension Day, Corpus Christi Day, the Thursday after 10 October, and 11 December.

The beadle was about the streets wearing his blue and scarlet coat with large yellow buttons and matching waistcoat, black breeches, knee buckles, shoe buckles, and, on special occasions, gold laced cocked hat and staff of office. At night, the watchman patrolled the dark streets.

In 1821, Ross had a population of 2,957 living in 585 houses. A dispensary was established in 1825 and in the same decade there was a post office opposite The Swan Inn. The Ross and Archenfield Bank was established in the Market Place in 1819 by John Jones, Nathaniel Morgan and Kedgwin Hoskins, and their integrity led to ten Herefordshire persons of property coming forward as guarantors and saving the bank in 1825-26 when many county banks suspended payment. A more colourful version is the family tradition that Morgan displayed a model farm wagon full of sovereigns, which restored confidence in the bank.

The Ross Bank at the corner of what is now St Mary's Street also survived, and later in the century the town was to have its own building society, the Ross and Archenfield, which developed land and allocated loans by ballot.

The provision of amenities and services was given impetus when the Royal Assent was given in 1830 to an Act for 'paving, cleaning, draining, regulating and improving the town of Ross and for disposing of certain common and waste lands and rights of common within the parish of Ross'.

The Act appointed as Commissioners the Lord of the Manor, the Rector, the Mayor or Sergeant at Mace, and named John Cooke, Nathaniel Morgan, Stratford Collins, Thomas Prichard, Edward Prichard, Richard Evans and all others who might fulfil qualifications of residence and rates.

There was no limit on the number of Commissioners and at a meeting on 24 October, 1837 there were no fewer that 25 present. This meeting anticipated by 20 years the establishment of a county constabulary, by taking action to protect the inhabitants and all passing through the town and 'for the purpose of putting an immediate stop to the disgraceful and unlawful proceedings which occur in the streets, particularly in the letting off of guns, pistols and fireworks'.

A motion to appoint two policemen was defeated, but a committee of five was set up to ascertain the best site for a lock-up house. A subscription list was opened but not until ten months later did the Commissioners agree that the lock-up should be in New Street and accepted a price of £180 for its building.

In the same month, August 1838, the Commissioners wrote to Colonel Rowen, of the London Police, asking him to send a 'proper policeman' with a view to appointment. In response came James Torrington Partridge, who in October told the Commissioners that he would not undertake to keep the town in order during the winter unless he had two policemen to assist him. The Commissioners agreed, on the understanding that the services of one policeman might be dispensed with in the spring! They opened yet another subscription list to find his wages. Sergeant Partridge, as he now became, was to be paid 30s a week until lodgings were found, and then 28s, and the constables 16s, with clothes in addition.

The Commissioners' relations with their newly-acquired Police Force do not appear to have been happy, for during the winter a resolution was put that the police should be directed by a committee, but as no one was prepared to serve on the committee the resolution was dropped. In the spring, the Commissioners lost no time in putting into effect their resolution of the previous autumn that the services of one policeman should be dispensed with at the end of the winter. In fact they went further; they decided to get rid of two, including Sergeant Partridge. The services of a constable named Harrison were retained; he was to live at the lock-up and be paid £1 a week plus the cost of three tons of coal.

The town's only fire-fighting appliances were wooden tanks on wheels, that had been kept in the north porch of the parish church since 1809. On Thursday 15 April, 1852, large numbers of men fought unsuccessfully to prevent fire destroying 30 acres of Chase Wood and early next morning the need for a proper fire engine became even more desperate. Fire engulfed the premises in New Street of the Ross and Forest of Dean Bank and the offices of Hall and Minett. Henry Minett, his wife and six children, governess and cook, were all brought by ladders to safety, but a 17-year-old maid servant, Emma Bird, died.

Hundreds of men and women formed lines up and down the street, bringing water from house pumps and rain butts, and hogsheads were brought by horse and trap. Still the fire raged. The brigade from Llandinabo took an hour to arrive and that from Hereford two hours. The Ross appliances were useless. Several times the engines had to be stopped while the leather piping was bound with handkerchiefs in an attempt to stop the water escaping.

The inquest jury expressed regret that the engines were in such a bad state of repair, and immediately a public suscription was mounted to buy a new engine. This was obtained the following September and was described as being of no ordinary powers.

The 1830 Act also required the Commissioners to provide lighting for the town, either by oil or gas, and they voted for the latter, though one complained 'the public money had better be thrown in the river than squandered in such a way'.

The Commissioners had the gas works in Kyrle Street in production by 1832, but 30 years later the undertaking had become incapable of meeting the needs of the town. The Commissioners, reluctant to raise more capital for expansion, obtained powers through the Ross Improvement Act of 1865 to sell the undertaking for £2,025 to James Harris, of Hanwell, Middlesex. On Harris's death in 1888, the Commissioners, regretting their earlier action, sought to buy the undertaking back, but the Harris family formed a limited company and retained possession until 1936 when the Severn Gas Company took the controlling interest. Nationalisation followed in 1949 and in 1955 manufacture of gas at Ross ceased, with the supply becoming integrated into the network of the South Western Gas Board.

The Ross Improvement Act, which received the Royal Assent on 19 June 1865, was concerned with other weighty matters — including the purchase of the Market House. Poultry, butter and other produce were sold in the streets until 1862 when the Ross Corn Exchange and Public Buildings Company Ltd, formed under the aegis of the Town Commissioners, provided a covered market.

When the Lord of the Manor, Kingsmill Manley Power, stepped in to claim the right to all tolls at the markets and title to the Market House, the Commissioners entered into a contract to purchase these and the pound adjoining the Royal Hotel stables for £1,000 and the Act found it expedient to confirm this.

Cattle and other livestock were also being sold in the streets and the Act empowered the Commissioners to provide a market, which they did at Homs Road in 1871. Nearly 100 years later, this market, which since 1927 had been held on Tuesdays, was at a low ebb, but the change in 1968 to a Friday market saw a dramatic reversal of fortunes.

From a market of 500 fat cattle and 16,000 sheep a year, it had grown by 1979 to one of 75,000 head of sheep, 8,000 fat cattle, 5,500 store cattle, with an annual turnover worth some £5 million.

The 1865 Act gave the Commissioners power to improve the water supply. Since the days of John Kyrle, the brook at the Rope Walk had turned the wooden wheel to pump water from the river to the Prospect, from where it was carried through mains of elm trees bored through the centre. When the river was more than half bank full or when the brook was low, the wheel would not work; the water was never fit for drinking, being taken from a point below the sewage outfall.

Many houses relied on wells, and when in 1859 the Commissioners placed an iron drinking bowl at the public pump at the Market Place, the water there was described as the best in town. For two decades the Commissioners discussed the water supply. In 1880 they were told that 353 of the 792 houses in the town had no water, 126 received the river supply and 19 were on a supply provided by Joseph Turnock from a lake at his house at Merrivale.

The problem was eventually solved by Thomas Blake, who in 1887 provided a wholesome supply from the artesian wells at Alton Court, which was pumped to the reservoir on Penyard before going by gravitation to the entire town. The soft water supply from the river was maintained and was extensively used by the laundry, brewery, and railway locomotives until the pumping station near The Hope and Anchor was closed in the mid-20th century.

Ross Water Undertaking, owned by the Blake family and with statutory powers, was merged into the Herefordshire Water Board in 1960. This board in turn was absorbed by the mammoth Welsh Water Authority in 1974.

Another health hazard to occupy the attention of the Commissioners was the keeping of pigs. The Medical Officer, Dr C. C. Cocks, reported in 1880 that 263 pigs were being kept in the town. There were 19 in High Street, four in Broad Street and no fewer than 52 in Brookend Street. Commissioners complained about the stench, but not wishing to impose undue hardship, took no decisive steps, though within a few years the keeping of pigs in the populated areas was to be prohibited.

Other provisions of the Ross Improvement Act included limiting the number of Commissioners to nine, to be elected by the male ratepayers, and giving authority for levying rates not exceeding two shillings and sixpence on the annual value of the property. Houses more than 100 yards from a public light were to be assessed at only one quarter of the yearly value.

In 1869, the Improvement Act was amended to incorporate the provision of the Towns' Police Clauses Act, 1847, and the Lords and Commons waived their fees for this amendment.

Until 1873, the town was ringed with turnpike gates administered by trustees. The tolls became increasingly unpopular; the people of Ashfield complained at having to pay every time they went through the gate at the top of Copse Cross Street and country people could see no reason why, having paid for the upkeep of their own roads, they should have to contribute to those in Ross. But when the trustees decided to abolish the tolls there was opposition from townspeople, who argued that it was not only they who used the streets. The trustees and the Town Commissioners, however, were concerned at the adverse effects the tolls were having on the market, and on 1 January, 1873, the turnpikes were abolished. Some tollhouses were sold by auction and others demolished for road widening.

Ross now had two newspapers. The earliest in the town was the *Ross and Archenfield Gazette,* printed by Thomas Farror in High Street, and which in its first issue on 9 June, 1855, recorded the opening of the Hereford-Ross-Gloucester railway line. The paper lasted only a few weeks, but long enough to describe the rejoicings that greeted the news of the fall of Sebastopol when 'every house in the town, both great and small,, exhibited such an amount of light in their windows that was never seen in Ross before. The town appeared in a blaze of light'.

Only four weeks after the launching of the town's first newspaper came a second, *The Man of Ross,* which was published for over 35 years. From 1867, readers had a choice, when William Enoch Hill founded the *Ross Gazette* which now after 112 years continues in the ownership of a private company. In 1903 came the *Ross Weekly News,* which was printed in Ledbury but was shortlived. In 1969 Berrows Newspapers launched the *Ross-on-Wye Advertiser.* So now, in an era when many larger towns do not have a newspaper of their very own, Ross has two, published within a few hours of each other every Wednesday.

The Ross dispensary had for many years been housed in New Street, and in 1872 rooms there were converted into wards to provide a cottage hospital. In 12 months it treated 26 patients and the need for larger premises soon became evident. A bequest of £1,000 by a vicar of Goodrich, the Rev H. C. Morgan, enabled the present Cottage Hospital to be built in 1879.

It has always held a warm place in the hearts of the population and this was in no way deterred by the 'nationalisation' of 1948 when its management went out of the hands of local governors. In two big efforts in the 1970s, the town, led by the Rotary Club, has provided the hospital with a casualty unit and a physiotherapy unit.

The community feeling is also extended towards Dean Hill Hospital for geriatrics and the sub-normal, in a building which was a workhouse for over 150 years from its erection in 1788.

Most of the public services down the years have been designed to meet the needs of the town exclusively, but the weather observatory started by Henry Southall in 1859 became in 1920 a first order synoptic station, supplying information to the whole of Europe. Information was transmitted from the Observatory in Crossfields six times a day until Frederick Parsons, who had succeeded Mr Southall in 1914, retired in 1974 at the age of 82. Attempts to keep it in being failed and it finally closed on 31 July, 1975.

The Town Commissioners gave way to the urban district council in 1895 and for the next 80 years a council of twelve directed the town's affairs, building hundreds of houses, maintaining the district roads, looking after the markets, providing amenities, and in 1956 constructing a sewage disposal works to bring to an end the unsalubrious habit of pouring untreated sewage into the river.

In February, 1939, the Corn Exchange was destroyed by fire and the produce, butter, and live and dressed poultry sales returned to the Market House. The inconvenience, accompanied by the outbreak of war and the consequent shortages, caused the market to dwindle rapidly. Soon the produce could be held on just two trestle tables and in 1953 the auctioneer's hammer fell for the last time, though the stalls still give the Market House and its surrounds an animated setting every Thursday and Saturday.

In 1974, the town's government passed to the South Herefordshire District Council, covering the area formerly administered by four authorities. Ross Town Council came into being with the powers only of a parish council, but with its chairman accorded the title of Mayor — thus reviving an office that had gone out of existence 95 years before on the death of the last holder, Mr Perris, in 1879.

The District Council administered their area covering more than half of Herefordshire from Woodside on the edge of Ross, but in 1979 moved to new headquarters at Hereford, bringing to an end nearly 1,000 years of administration in the town.

Ancient Ross seen from Cawdor.

32

ABOVE: A print from Cornelius Varley's painting of the Market Place in 1803. BELOW: The old Market Place is still the centre of much activity on Thursdays and Saturdays.

ROSS TOWN ACT.

NOTICE

Is hereby given that persons willing to agree with the Commissioners for the repairing and cleansing of all the Streets within the Town of Ross, for one or three years, to commence on the 1st day of March next: if for one year, at a sum not exceeding £75, and if for three years, at a sum not exceeding £70 per annum, must send in sealed Tenders to my Offices, on or before the 11th of February next.

AND NOTICE is hereby also given that persons willing to agree for the taking up and laying down of certain Street Crossings, in the said Town, are requested in like manner to send in Tenders.

FULL particulars on both the before mentioned subjects, may be obtained on application to me, good security, to the satisfaction of the Commissioners, will be required in each of the above cases, for the due fulfillment of the contracts to be entered into, and the Commissioners do not, in either affair, pledge themselves to accept the lowest Tender.

Wm. POWELL HOOPER,
Clerk to the said Commissioners.

Dated 16th January, 1850.

ABOVE LEFT: Alton (formerly Old Town) Street. RIGHT: Minutes of the Court Leet for 12 October, 1790, when the business was to elect the Mayor and other officials. Three names were put forward for each post and members voted by putting ticks against each name. BELOW LEFT: The cost of public services in 1850. RIGHT: Henry Southall, 1826-1916.

34

ABOVE: The old gaol in new Street. BELOW: Superintendent Frederick John Hackford Broad and other guardians of the law, pictured about 60 years ago in the yard of the old police station at the foot of Brampton Street.

35

RULES AND REGULATIONS

for the

ROSS FIRE BRIGADE.

The Brigade will be under the direction of a Committee elected from the Town Commissioners.

The Brigade will consist of fourteen men, viz.:—The Captain; an Engineer, who will also act as the Foreman of the Brigade; Twelve Firemen; and two men whose duty it will be to attend to the suction, or other supply of water.

The Captain must be well acquainted with the principle and construction of the force-pump and fire-engine. He must be accustomed to Engine work;

The Engine, and everything connected with it, will be under the special care of the Captain, or whom he may appoint; and it will be his duty to see that everything is in its place, and that the Engine is always ready for action.

The Firemen must be men accustomed to work on ladders, and ascend heights. Carpenters and Masons are to be preferred. When a vacancy occurs, the Brigade will fill it by electing another member; but the Committee may set aside the election if the individual chosen be deemed an unfit person.

The Brigade men who attend to the suction must make themselves acquainted with the various pumps, wells, and private cisterns of large size, which exist in the town. It is also very desirable that they should be well acquainted with the town water-works, and be able to direct the best respecting the best way of obtaining a good supply from that source in case of fire. The Committee are of opinion that it is desirable that the Fire Brigade should consist of men under 50 years of age, and that they should be efficient mechanics.

The helmets of the Firemen will be numbered from 1 to 12; but these numbers are merely for convenience, and are not intended to denote any difference in rank.

When riding on the Engine, the Captain and Engineer will take the driver's seat; No. 1 will sit first on the left hand side, then 2, 3, 4, 5, 6; No. 7 will sit first on the right hand side with 8, 9, 10, 11, and 12; the Brigade men who attend to the suction sitting behind.

No. 1, or the Fireman who supplies his place, will always mount the Engine to give out the hose to the rest; he will begin with No. 2 on the left side, and No. 8 on the right.

The first man on the right side will take the branch pipe first.

Each member of the Brigade will be furnished with a helmet, axe, and belt. It is hoped that these articles will be kept safely, used only in the service of the Brigade, and must be returned to the Captain when any individual wishes to withdraw from the body.

Occasional practice being absolutely necessary, it is earnestly requested that no one will enter the Brigade who is unwilling to join in the required exercise.

In all cases of fire, the Town Hall Bell will be rung to summon the Brigade.

No man is to be accounted a Fireman, or paid for his attendance at a Fire, who has not attended practice during the year. Should a Fire occur early in the year, the attendance of the previous year will of course be deemed sufficient.

The Committee would suggest that all persons requiring the Fire Engine should send a written order for same.

The following are the charges which will be made for the use of the Engine and the service of the Fire Brigade:—

	£	s.	d.
For the use of the Engine within the four first mile-posts	4	4	0
For every mile or portion of mile beyond the four mile-post from Ross	0	10	6
For every Brigade man who shall be present when the Engine commences working, and continues with the Engine until dismissed by the Captain—in the Town	0	4	6
Ditto, ditto, in the Country	0	7	6

Drivers, 7s. 6d.; after seven hours, 1s. per hour.

If engaged more than seven hours in the Country or three hours in the Town, each man so engaged will be paid 1s. per hour.

All expenses incurred in the conveyance of the Engine to fires, and back to Ross, are to be paid by the parties requiring the use of the same.

William Hill, Steam Printer, Gazette Office, High Street, Ross.

ROSS FIRE BRIGADE

THIS STEAM FIRE ENGINE

WAS PURCHASED BY PUBLIC SUBSCRIPTION
SUPPLEMENTED BY A GRANT FROM THE

RURAL DISTRICT COUNCIL

AND HANDED OVER TO THE

ROSS URBAN COUNCIL
AND FIRE BRIGADE

SEPTEMBER. 1899.

FREDERICK COOPER. J.P. CHAIRMAN OF COMMITTEE
H.T. BLAKE. CHIEF OFFICER OF FIRE BRIGADE
H.J. BIRD. *LIEUTENANT.* A.BIRD *ENGINEER.*

FIREMEN

C.BIRD. J.BAILEY. C.WHITBY. W.WAITES. T.GARDNER.
T.COUNSELL. L.MORGAN. J.MARSHALL. T.BAYNHAM.
T.YEMM. H.PEACOCK. E.HILL. H.BROOKS. E.BLAKE.

LEFT: One hundred years ago those needing the services of the Fire Brigade were advised to send a written order. RIGHT: Plaque on the steam fire engine.

Pride in a job well done: the completion of the Post Office in 1899. (Photo: R. E. Davies).

ABOVE: Ross fire engine and crew in the early years of this century. (Photo: R. E. Davies). INSET: A cheque of the Ross and Archenfield Bank, which was in the Market Place. BELOW: The model of a Herefordshire farm wagon that tradition says was filled with gold sovereigns to restore confidence in the Ross and Archenfield Bank in the crises of 1825-6. The model, 14 inches long, 7 inches wide and 3½ inches deep, is now in the possession of R. Nicholas Stephens of Sidmouth, Devon.

THE
Ross and Archenfield
AND GENERAL ADVERTISE

No. 1.   SATURDAY, JUNE 9, 1855.

ROSS.

VALUABLE FREEHOLD PROPERTY.

TO BE SOLD BY AUCTION,

By MORGAN & SON,

At BARRETT'S ROYAL HOTEL, in the Town of Ross, on MONDAY, the 18th of JUNE, 1855, at Six o'clock in the Afternoon, subject to conditions of sale to be then produced, in one or more lots, as may be agreed on :—

ALL that commodious DWELLING-HOUSE, called "VAGA PLACE," together with the extensive Yards, Stables, and Garden, thereto adjoining and belonging.

These commodious premises are situated at the Dock Pitch, Ross ; and the House, which is in excellent repair, was some time since used as a Ladies' Boarding School, and lately in the occupation of Messrs. Peto, Brassey, and Betts, whose term expired at the opening of the Hereford, Ross, and Gloucester Railway.

The House contains three Sitting-rooms, and a large Dining-room, 30ft. by 16ft., eight Bed-rooms, Kitchen, extensive Cellarage, &c., &c.

It has two entrances, and may be used as two Houses, is delightfully and healthily situated, commanding beautiful prospects of the River Wye and Neighbourhood.

The property is admirably adapted for the erection of a Factory or Brewery, being near to the River Wye and the Water Works, with the advantage of Railway communication to all parts of the Kingdom. One-half of the purchase-money may remain on mortgage, if wished ; and immediate possession can be had.

☞ For particulars, apply to MESSRS. COLLINS, Solicitors, Ross ; and to view the property, to the AUCTIONEERS, Ross.

WALFORD, HEREFORDSHIRE.

DESIRABLE FREEHOLD ESTATE,

Near the Banks of the Wye.

TO BE SOLD BY AUCTION,

By MORGAN & SON,

On WEDNESDAY, the 13th day of JUNE, 1855, at the GEORGE INN, in the Town of Ross, at Five o'Clock in the Afternoon, in Four Lots, subject to conditions to be then produced.

LOT 1.—

ALL that newly-erect... ...built

The Houses are well supplied with water. The Land is in a high state of cultivation, commands varied and extensive views of the River Wye and surrounding picturesque country, is on good roads, within three miles of the Ross Station on the Hereford, Ross, and Gloucester Railway, and near to Coal and Lime. Excellent Stone may be raised upon the Estate for building purposes.

This Property adjoins lands of J. Partridge, Esq., K. M. Power, Esq., Mr. John Hardwick, Mr. James Whiting, Mr. Philip Jones, and Mr. William Young.

Immediate possession of the Queach House may be had, and possession of the Land may be had on the 29th September next.

For further particulars, apply to Messrs. Heffill and Barnard, Solicitors, Dis... ...e Messrs. Sharpe, Field, and Jacks... ...dford-row, London ; or to the ... ...will appoint a person to sh... ...he Estate may be seen at...

CORPS-C...

MORGAN and ... on the abov... DAY, the 11th and ... of the STOCK-I... NITURE, and ... tatives of Mr. I...

The Stock-in-... will be sold the ... Furniture, &c., ...

☞ Sale a...

ADVA... ...HE TI...

...BARR...

To Coach...

Im...

CARRIA...

MORGAN ... Mr. Bar... Hereford, R... by AUCTIC... THURSDAY, t... seasoned HO... and colors, po... off the Mails... HARNESS, ... Five 5-years'-... SES AND M... (never worke... and likely to...

The Sale w... tually.

Catalogue... EL, and the ... Broad-Str...

OR SAI... Broadw... od tone. Apply at ... ffice ; or to ... road Street,

...HE PUB...

...W. FREEM...

...IGH STREET, ROSS,

Will make no alteration in the price of Teas, ex...

ONE TRIAL WILL PROVE THIS TO BE THE CHEAPEST AND BES...

AGENTS FOR

The first edition of the *Ross and Archenfield Gazette,* 9 June 1855. INSET: William Enoch Hill (1833-1891) who founded the *Ross Gazette* in 1867.

ABOVE: Support for Roberts, the Conservative candidate, in a 1920s General Election campaign. BELOW: The final meeting of Ross Urban District Council on 25 March, 1974.

ABO
paris.
unde
sun r
in 19

...y of Rudhall Manor in 1890. It stands at the junction of three
...nt parts being at Ross, Brampton Abbotts and Weston-
...LEFT: Chasedale Weather Observatory, 1914-1921. The
...form can be seen on the roof. RIGHT: Crossfields took over
...ed in 1975. This apparatus recorded hours of sunshine and
temperature.

Cap. cviii.

An Act for more effectually paving, lighting, and improving the Town of *Ross* in the County of *Hereford*, for maintaining and providing Markets within such Town, and for supplying the same with Water; and other Purposes.

[19th *June* 1865.]

WHEREAS by the Act (Local) Eleventh *George* the Fourth, Chapter Forty-three, a Body of Commissioners (in this Act called " the existing Commissioners ") was appointed, and the District, as defined by the said Act, was paved, drained, lighted, and otherwise improved: And whereas the existing Commissioners became possessed of Gasworks and Plant, and Mains and Pipes connected therewith, for the Purpose of supplying the said District with Gas: And whereas the said Works being found altogether insufficient, and the existing Commissioners being unable from Want of Funds to make the necessary Additions to the same, determined, for the Benefit and Convenience of the Inhabitants of the said District, to sell the said Works, and they accordingly contracted to sell the said Works and the other Hereditaments and Premises held therewith, and their Plant, Mains, and Pipes, in consideration of the

11 G. 4. & i W. 4. c. xliii.

[*Local.*]   16 *C*   Sum

ABOVE: The 1865 Ross Improvement Act. BELOW: Palace Close at the end of the 19th century.

ABOVE: Ross Urban District Council in 1910. BELOW: The scene at the Market House in October, 1899, when Dorothy Moffat (later Mrs Guy Trafford) christened the fire engine *The John Kyrle*.

"EVERY MAN HIS OWN LANDLORD."

PROSPECTUS

OF THE

ROSS & ARCHENFIELD BENEFIT BUILDING,

FREEHOLD LAND AND INVESTMENT SOCIETY.

The grand objects contemplated by this Society, are—to improve the Social, promote the Moral, and exalt the Political Condition of the Industrious Classes ; by securing to each of its members the enviable possession—obtained by his own industry and frugality—of a Freehold which he may enjoy himself, and afterwards leave unencumbered to his posterity, and on which he may either erect a dwelling, cultivate as a garden, or let to a tenant ; consequently, it deserves the support of all who are friendly to these objects, and are desirous of reducing the burden of Poor Rates, by enabling every careful and industrious man, to provide for his own necessities.

It is a lamentable fact, that many of the Working Classes who once possessed a little property, have lost it either through misfortune, or, too frequently, their own negligence and improvidence. This Society will counteract such evils by affording working men a stimulus to exertion, and the cultivation of good habits, where other means have failed. It will thus not only give to those who deserve it and to whom it may safely be entrusted—a voice in the National Councils, but will at the same time teach them to practise a spirit of economy, industry, self-dependence, and consequently self-respect,—making them better citizens and better men ; and, while it gives to such the political franchise, it will in no way interfere in its free exercise, so that persons of all shades of political opinion may freely participate in its benefits. The Society proposes to effect these objects by means of a fund accumulated by the weekly contributions of its members, and of borrowed capital when necessary, which will be economically laid out in the purchase of estates or large tracts of land, as conveniently situated as possible, which will be divided among its members at cost price, according to priority of membership ; there will be no bidding for shares, or distribution by lot, and consequently no chance of failure ; every member will receive the full value of his subscriptions, and when the price is paid up, will have its full equivalent restored to him.

To persons desirous of investing either large or small sums, none offer .... on all subscriptions and deposits, which is augmented when the funds are i.........................

Few individuals form an adequate conception of the immense advantag....................... the following fact will make it manifest : the Freehold Land Society, in Bir........................ for small portions of which 3s 3d. per square yard had been refused. The p......................... all the members, land worth 40s. a year for about £30 ; it thus gives the poo........................ited to his wants at the same rate as the rich man buys a large estate, which..........................

The subscription of every member will commence when he joins the S................... the cost of his Allotment and Transfer. A member may pay any amount of .... pay the remainder and have the property at once conveyed to him, instead of ....iety will cease, but may be renewed by his taking fresh shares.

In times of depression, or in case of sickness, any member may suspen.....................raw from the Society altogether, either by disposing of his share with interest ....d in. In case of death his representative or next of kin takes the share.

Ross and Archenfield

FREEHOLD LAND AND

BENEFIT BUILDING SOCIETY.

The Third Anniversary of this Society

WILL BE CELEBRATED BY A PUBLIC

TEA MEETING

IN THE TOWN HALL, ROSS,

ON MONDAY, THE 3rd of JANUARY, 1853,

AT FIVE O'CLOCK IN THE AFTERNOON.

Addresses will be delivered by several friends of the cause ; and the propriety of establishing a FRIENDLY SOCIETY, on improved principles, will be discussed.

TICKETS TO THE TEA 1s. EACH. ADMISSION AT 7 O'CLOCK FREE.

ROSS : PRINTED BY R. POW.E & SONS, "STAMP-OFFICE."

The mode of allotment will be as follows ; when Land is purchased b..........................de it into lots, or shares, worth at least 40s. per annum ; these lots, supposing them to be 50, are offered to the members good upon the books according to seniority of membership, until a sufficient number signify their wish to accept them ; the lots are then numbered and balloted for among such shareholders, and the deeds, prepared by the Society's Solicitor, are held by the Trustees till the shareholder has paid up the cost of his allotment.

The Society being enrolled as a Benefit Building Society is exempt from Stamp Duties, and has the power of advancing money to its members to purchase or erect a dwelling house or houses, or for the redemption of mortgages ; thus combining a Building Society and Freehold Land Society, and managing both departments at the cost of one.

Entrance Fee, 1s. per share. Subscription, 1s. 0½d. per share, per week. Transfer Fee, 1s. per share. No Fine on withdrawal. Members may take any number of shares not exceeding six : and may have their allotments together, or separate ; and may reside in any part of the country ; Minors and Females, and persons of any political principles, are admitted Shareholders. Members at a distance will have property purchased near their own residences, if preferred, whenever a suitable opportunity offers.

Prospectus for the Ross and Archenfield Benefit Building Society. INSET:
Advertisement for a meeting of the Ross and Archenfield Benefit Building
Society, Monday 3 January, 1853.

44

TO THE
INHABITANTS OF ROSS.

At a meeting of the TOWN COMMISSIONERS, held 13th March, 1849, the new site for the GAS WORKS was brought under consideration, and a proposal made to give Mr. Cooke of the Chase £200 for an acre of his land called the Mill-tail pleck, with interest at five per cent until paid, as explained below.

The Commissioners to erect a suitable Bridge over the Mill-tail stream within the first year.

To make, and stone, a Carriage road, to join the Homs road, by the end of the second year.

To fence off the ground, and pay the purchase money for the Land, by the end of the fourth year.

That Mr. Cooke might have the option of taking to shares in the new Gas Works, at twenty pounds each, or at such other sum as should be determined upon, instead of the purchase money.

That the Shareholders might receive interest not exceeding six per cent. on the outlay, the remaining profit from the concern to go towards liquidating any debts that might be incurred in erecting the Gas Works, or otherwise.

The following Gas estimates may be acceptable as quoted from various works.

Cr.	£	s.	d.
200 Tons of Coals will make *1,840,000 feet of Gas, at 10s. per thousand is .	†920	0	0
16 Chaldrons of Breese from 200 Tons of Coals, at 10s. per Chaldron . .	3	4	0
2000 Gallons of Tar from 200 Tons of Coals, at 1d. per Gallon . . .	8	6	8
100 Tons of Coke from 200 Tons of Coals at 5s per Ton	25	0	0
Total	£956	10	8

Dr.			
200 Tons of Coals, at 10s. per Ton	100	0	0
Wages for two Men	126	0	0
Wear and Tear of Works per annum	100	0	0
Lime and bad Debts	60	0	0
Rates and Taxes per annum - - - - - - - -	10	10	8
£1000, if borrowed on the Works, at 6 per cent - - - - - -	60	0	0
	456	10	8
Net profit	500	0	0

	£	s.	d.
Should Gas be sold at 8s. per thousand feet, say - - -	762	6	8
But if at 6s. per ditto, say - - - - - - -	588	6	8

Or 460 Private Lights, and each light to burn 4000 feet of Gas per year, is *1,840,000 feet. } is - †920 0 0
Or 460 Private Lamps, and each †£2 per annum, - }

Proposals of the Ross Town Commissioners, 13 March, 1849.

The Man of Ross,

AND GENERAL ADVERTISER FOR THE COUNTIES OF HEREFORD, GLOUCESTER, AND MONMOUTH.

PRINTED AND PUBLISHED, EVERY THURSDAY MORNING, BY J. W. F. COUNSELL, MARKET PLACE, ROSS.

No. 219.   THURSDAY, SEPTEMBER 8, 1859.   ONE PENNY.

GENERAL STATEMENT

Of all Moneys received and paid by virtue or in execution of the Ross Improvement Act, from the 2nd Day of July, 1861, to the 1st day of July, 1862.

Income.

	£	s.	d.
Balance in Treasurer's hands brought from last Statement	1	16	8
„ in the hands of the Gas Committee	6	1	2½
„ in the hands of the Surveyor	0	19	11
„ collected of Rate granted 13th September, 1859	1	3	10
„ ditto ditto 24th April, 1860	5	4	7½
„ of Rate granted 20th November, 1860 ... 83 13 10½			
Uncollected, excused, and void ... 60 11 6¼	23	2	4
Amount of Rate granted 14th May, 1861 ... 318 14 7			
Uncollected, excused, and void ... 64 7 0	254	7	7
Amount of Rate granted 10th December, 1861 ... 319 2 2			
Uncollected, excused, and void ... 83 18 8½	235	3	5½
Amount collected for Gas, Coke, Lime, Tar, and Fittings	732	19	9½
„ One Quarter's Gas for lighting 54 Public Lamps	27	0	0
Manure sold	9	12	0
Amount received for Paving, &c.	6	2	9
„ Returned overpaid Income Tax	2	16	7
Balance due to Surveyor and Collector	0	4	10
	£1306	**15**	**7**
Balance in Treasurer's hands brought down	2	10	1
„ In the hands of the Gas Committee	1	13	8½

Expenditure.

	£	s.	d.
Paid accounts for repairing Streets, Highways, Gutters, Drains, Stone and Brick, &c	82	15	1½
„ Footways, Paving and Pitching	48	6	10
„ As per Labor Book for Scavengering, Hauling, breaking Stone and other Labor	99	19	1
„ Keep of Horse	41	14	11
„ Incidental Expences	3	2	10
„ Wages for making Gas, superintendence, and collection of Gas money, &c.	123	12	0
„ For Coal, Lime, and Sand, for Manufacture of Gas	339	0	0
„ For alterations of Retorts, Gas Meters, and Fittings	141	2	0
„ Tradesmen's Bills, Sundries, Carriage, &c.	39	15	4½
„ For Labor, lighting Lamps, &c.	18	0	0
„ One Year's Interest on Mortgage money	22	10	0
„ Amount paid to credit at Bank, difference between Cash drawn out and Cash paid in	80	7	11
„ Quarter's Rent for Gas, lighting Public Lamps	27	0	0
„ Poors Rate and Income Tax	19	10	1½
„ For Patent Gullies	6	18	0
„ Mr. Henry Richardson, putting back Window	5	0	0
„ Mr. M. O. Overton ditto	10	0	0
„ Mr. John Treherne, compensation as to One Mill Garden	6	0	0
„ Pump repairs	8	8	6
„ Law business	2	4	5
„ Expences of Firemen at Blackhouse, &c., (to be repaid by Mr. Wm. Badham)	2	18	8
„ One Year's Rent Manure deposit, to 2nd February, 1862	3	0	0
„ Printing	1	19	6
„ On account of taking down Middle Row to widen Street ... *Under Helle*	100	0	0
„ Superintendent of Police inspecting Common Lodging Houses	5	0	0
„ Labels for Street Names, Painting and Lettering	5	19	0
„ Rent of Stable, and Fire Engine House	11	2	6
„ Clerk's Year's Salary	20	0	0
„ Treasurer's ditto	5	5	0
„ Surveyor, Collector, and Scavenger's Salary	22	0	0
„ Balance in the hands of the Gas Committee	1	13	8½
„ In Treasurer's hands	2	10	1
	£1306	**15**	**7**
Balance brought down due to Collector, and Surveyor	0	4	10
Amount of Debts now owing by Commissioners, on account of Gas Works, (about)	44	0	0
Amount of other Debts (about)	40	0	0

8th July, 1862.   Examined and settled at a General Annual Meeting of the Commissioners.

(Signed)   F. H. ADAMS, Chairman.
THOMAS BLAKE.
BENJN. BRUNSDON.
JOSEPH TURNOCK.
THOS. DONNE.
WALTER FREEMAN.
D. F. COLLINS.

PRINTED AT THE OFFICE OF WILLIAM HILL, PRINTER AND STATIONER, ROSS.

ABOVE: *The Man of Ross,* Thursday 8 September, 1859. BELOW: The Ross Improvement Act accounts, dated 8 July, 1862, shows £100 spent on the taking down of Under Helle (Middle Row).

Prayer and Persecution

The church of St Mary the Virgin, built in the decorated style, is possibly the third parish church in the history of the town. There was a Saxon church and traces of chalky rock in the exterior wall of the chancel suggest that there was a Norman church. A lightly-held tradition is that this church was destroyed in the civil strife between the armies of Stephen and Matilda.

The first known rector was William de Ablaniat, in 1287, three years after the building of the present church started. The chancel, nave and north and south aisles were all completed by the dedication in 1316. The south porch and tower also date from the early 14th century. In the latter part of the century the north porch was added and the chancel extended some 12 or 15ft to the east.

Besides the high altar, there were altars for St George and St Margaret, which were probably chantries. John de Rosse, Rector, in 1312 founded a chantry in honour of the Blessed Virgin and St Thomas the Martyr, endowing it with 74 acres of his land in Ross and Walford. The chantries all became impoverished through depredations on the estate.

Until the reign of Charles II, Ross had a rector and a vicar, the rectory being a sinecure of greater value than the vicarage, which included the chapels of neighbouring Weston-under-Penyard and Brampton Abbotts.

Thomas Chippenham, Vicar 1462-86, had a rood loft erected across the opening to the chancel. It was taken down more than 200 years ago but evidence of the altar on it is still to be found by the piscina high on the wall on the right of the chancel.

Vicar Philip Price was a courageous priest who ministered to the dying through the months of plague in 1637, and at 5 o'clock one morning led the townspeople through the streets chanting a litany with supplications for deliverance. The plague is said to have abated from that morning but Vicar Price's loyalty to his sovereign resulted in his being deprived of his living nine years later in the Civil War.

The side chapel was built in 1510 and in the 19th century had a gallery opening into the south aisle. Another gallery at the same time was at the west end, where the organ was placed. It is recorded that in 1851 the church had 1,400 sittings, 400 of which were free. Nowadays the churchwardens are hard pressed to find seats for a congregation of more than 400.

The glass providing the four lights in the east window dates from 1430 and was originally in the Bishop's palace at Stretton Sugwas. It was brought to Ross in the 18th century and placed in no particular order. After 100 years of disarray it was put back in its original form in 1873 by German glass experts who were working at St Weonards. The glass of the scroll above the figure on the left is modern and wrongly describes St Ethelbert as Edward the Confessor.

The greater part of the 14th century spire was rebuilt in 1721 through the zeal of The Man of Ross. Pinnacles were added to the tower at the same time. More than half of the spire was rebuilt after being struck by lightning on 12 July 1852. The top was rebuilt in 1911 and again in 1952, when the spire was slightly shortened to 205ft. Three of the four pinnacles were taken down in 1975 as a safety measure and have not yet been replaced.

Trees growing inside the church were a unique feature. Two were in the window at the east end of the north transept and another in the nearby window in the north wall. They were suckers from elms planted outside by John Kyrle and they came through the wall near his pew. When the parent trees were cut down in the extensive restoration of the church in 1878, the suckers died, but their remains stayed until 1953 when, riddled with woodworm, they had to be destroyed.

The organ was given by Mrs Edith Purchas as a thanks-offering at the end of the First World War. She died soon after its dedication in 1921 and hers was the first funeral at which the organ was played.

The high altar, though of Old English design, is of modern construction, being the parish's memorial to the Fallen of the Second World War. The Baptistry was given by Mr and Mrs J. W. Done as a memorial to their 15-year-old daughter who died suddenly when she was an evacuee from London in Ross in 1942. There is no memorial tablet, but a remembrance is the carving of a little girl's head on each of the kneeling desks.

The church's orientation is not to the traditional east, but is east-north-east, as is the plague cross in the churchyard.

The persecution of Roman Catholics in the 17th century fell hard on South Herefordshire. Priest John Kemble from St Weonards was hanged for his faith in 1679 and was canonised in 1970. In the more tolerant Victorian age, Roman Catholics held services at St Mary's Cottage in the Crofts; during the priesthood of Dr H. J. Marshall a church was built there. It is now the meeting place of Jehovah's Witnesses, for a new church was built with the legacy of Miss Frances Mary Webb on the corner of Sussex Avenue. It was blessed in 1931 by the Right Rev Mgr Irvine, Provost and Vicar General of the Archdiocese of Cardiff.

The United Reformed Church has its origins in the Independent Church founded in 1662 by the Rev Anthony Collier, who was ejected from his living in Gloucestershire because he would not assent to the Act of Uniformity.

The earliest meeting place is believed to be a warehouse in Copse Street; a 19th century minister, William Byrne, wrote, 'In those days it would seem that the people who preferred the ministry of Mr Collier to that of the parish priest were accustomed to assemble in a large upper room as did the disciples of Jerusalem'.

On Charles II issuing the Declaration of Indulgence in 1672, Collier became licensed to preach 'at his own house in Ross', and before Byrne took up his ministry in 1826, the congregation had acquired a chapel in Kyrle Street. Byrne averred that 'in coming to Ross he found the congregation nearly dissipated, the edifice almost a ruin, and many other things which called loudly for an instant and searching reform'. But he was also able to affirm that 'the Lord brought His servants through a fiery trial, enabled them to accomplish the end contemplated, and to put the place in thorough repair at an expense of several hundred pounds. Bless the Lord'.

On 3 March, 1848, the church united with the Congregational Union of England and Wales, and in 1864 the church meeting began to discuss a new building. The foundation stone of the present church in Gloucester Road was laid on 3 June, 1867, by H. O. Wills of Bristol and on 21 July of the following year, the church was opened by the Rev Newman Hill, of Surrey. In 1966, the Congregational Church united with the Presbyterian Church to become the United Reformed Church.

A founder of Methodism, Rev George Whitfield, came to Ross in 1743 and John Wesley subsequently made three visits. He was accompanied by his brother Charles on 16 February, 1749. On 9 August 1784, John recorded, 'I rode over the Malvern Hills which afford one of the finest prospects in the kingdom, to Ledbury, then through the miserable roads to Ross.' He had dinner at Ross on that occasion and tea on his third visit on 6 August 1790.

The first record of organised Methodism in Ross appeared in an article in the Wesleyan Methodist Magazine of 1835, which said, 'Methodism was introduced in Ross about 27 years ago and in the midst of much opposition existed fifteen years. About this time, the room in which the society worshipped was burned down and the most influential members left the place. The preaching was therefore discontinued and the society dissolved.'.

In 1830 another room was opened but again 'the persecution began to rage'. On 17 October 1834, a chapel was opened in Overross Street but though the congregations were so large that many had to stand, the chapel was inconvenient and noisy. This worsened when the building of the railway line in 1855 involved the erection of a bridge close to the chapel.

A new church was built in Edde Cross Street at a cost of £1,000, the foundation stone being laid by the Rev Morley Punshon on 4 June 1867. Soon after its centenary, an architect's report in 1970 showed that repairs would cost as much as the provision of a new building. The last service was held in June 1971, and the Methodists had the use of the Anglican Mission Room at Overross until the new church, built on the same site, was opened on 15 July 1972 by Paul Bartlett Lang, Secretary of the Joseph Rank Benevolent Trustees, who provided £13,000 of the cost of £21,000.

For more than 150 years, Baptists in the town journeyed three miles or so along the road to Gloucester for their Sunday worship in the hamlet of Ryeford. The chapel there, within the parish of Weston-under-Penyard, was founded by the rector, the Rev John Skinner, when he was ejected from his living in 1662.

It was not until 1818 that the 22 members from Ross decided to have their own church, to the dismay of the Ryeford Baptists. They acquired a site in Broad Street and opened a modest chapel there on 6 October 1819. As the years went by, the inadequacy of the little building was felt more and more and when the members were told that repairs would cost £400, they decided that now was the time to build a larger church on the same site. The final services in the old chapel were held on 10 April 1881, and so rapid was the work of demolition and rebuilding that the new church was opened on 6 December of the same year. The sermon on that great day was preached by Thomas Blake, who had contributed £3,162 16s 3d of the entire cost of £3,700.

The graveyard that had been provided at the rear of the original church was closed for burials in 1884.

Intolerance was also encountered by the brethren who laid the foundations for what is now the Henry Street Evangelical Church. Captain William Rhind was one of a group of Naval and military officers who had come together in Plymouth to hold meetings in New Testament simplicity — the Plymouth Brethren. In 1839 he moved to Hereford and every Sunday, after the morning service, would ride on horseback to Ross to spread the teaching. He conducted services on the Market House steps and it was said that his powerful, clear, sonorous voice could be heard in Brookend Street.

On one occasion the town band was enlisted to interrupt the service. They played some lively pieces while Rhind, Bible in hand, patiently waited. Eventually, he quietly said, 'Friends, when you have done I will begin'. Shamefacedly, the musicians stole away.

In 1843, he made his home in Ross, where it was not uncommon to see a couple of men stripped to the waist and fighting in the street, while a crowd goaded them on. Whenever he heard of this happening, Rhind would hurry to the spot and in a tone blending love and authority, he would stand between the opponents saying, 'My dear friends, I cannot allow you to injure yourselves'. Often, this stopped the fighting. A man who was reputed to be the champion fighter of Ross, Thomas Griffiths, nicknamed 'Bottler' because he bottled up his opponents so quickly, came under the power of this Christian man. He became a true believer and sometimes took part in the services.

From 1844, the Brethren were holding their meetings in a room in Wilton Road. It had accommodation for 130, but soon much more space was needed. The building was doubled but still this was not enough, and in 1856 a meeting house was opened in Station Street, with accommodation for more than 400. It was here that the funeral service was held for Captain Rhind, who died in 1863 at the age of 68. Christians of all denominations attended, and the body was taken by train to Hereford for burial, carried in a compartment lined with evergreens.

The Station Street hall was in use only nine years, for the Alton Court Brewery Company, whose premises filled much of the street, needed the site. Their offer to move the hall to Henry Street was accepted and the transaction completed in 1866.

Quakerism was quick to come to Ross and its members had a profound influence on the development of the town. In 1655, only eight years after George Fox had started touring the country preaching his message, two of his followers, Thomas Goodaire and George Scaife, arrived in Ross on foot from the north and found a congregation waiting to hear them 'in the steeple house'. After the meeting, James Merrick, a tanner, took the visitors to his home in the Market Place, where they met 'severall of ye new Convinced friends' and it was decided that a meeting should be held at the house 'every first day'. This arrangement continued until 1676 when the Ross Friends built their own meeting house at the foot of Brampton Street. It has a long walled-in entrance, typical of the meeting houses built during the persecution.

The Restoration of the Monarchy brought hard times for the Quakers. In 1661, a captain of the militia arrested 16 Friends for refusing to swear allegiance to Charles II (their objection was not to allegiance but to swearing). They were imprisoned in Hereford gaol for several months and though their gaoler was 'a very wicked and cruell' man, their resolute, yet calm, demeanour, won respect

The Book of (Quaker) Sufferings also records hard treatment given to two poor women at Ross: '1661. Frances Thomas, widow, five children under ten to provide for by the labour of her hands, and had very little of clothing or household stuff, Yet out of the poor remains of her goods, the cruel persecutors took a kettle worth 5s and a bolster worth 3s. Katherine Pritchard, aged 70 years. Having scarce any goods, the persecutors took a gown valued at 15s which she used to cover her with for want of bedclothes and for lack of it suffered much by cold in her extreme old age'.

George Fox himself attended a meeting at Merrick's house in 1663, and until this century it was known as 'Friends Place'.

The Toleration Act of 1689 eased the persecution, but between 1692 and 1796 at least 22 Ross Friends were distrained for varying amounts. Undaunted, the Friends were now beginning to take a full part in local affairs. Thomas Prichard, referred to in his obituary in 1843 as 'The Patriarch of Ross' was a promoter of the Lancastrian School first held in the Market House. He was the father of the distinguished James Cowles Prichard.

Nathaniel Morgan, 1775-1854, lived at Friends Place and opened there the Ross and Archenfeld Bank in 1819.

Morgan also conducted a drapery business at Friends Place and there he was joined in 1851 by a young Quaker, Henry Southall. The young man was appointed Treasurer of the Ross meeting and on Nathaniel's death in 1854 he became their Clerk. It was he who founded the weather observatory, and was Chairman of the Town Commissioners, the first Chairman of the Urban Council, a County Councillor, magistrate and botanist. On his death, tributes were paid to him at the parish church and Nonconformist churches and he was described as one of the most honoured and respected townsmen that Ross had ever known.

Mr Southall died in 1916 and in the same year the meeting house was closed because there was no one of sufficient authority to continue the meetings. After an interregnum of ten years it was revived in 1926, largely because of a colony of Friends who settled at

Parkfields, some three miles away, to develop the land on horticultural lines. In 1979, the Friends at Ross are once again down to a handful, and as this book goes to press, the meeting house is up for sale. The District Council has expressed preliminary interest, for the graveyard and gardens offer development potential and the meeting house building itself, could perhaps become a Heritage Centre or town community facilty. We must hope that this portion of Ross's past survives private speculation and despoliation and continues to serve the town.

The Salvation Army were most unwelcome when they held meetings in Ross in the early 1880s. The *Ross Gazette* often referred to them as 'The Sunday Nuisance' and one week reported, 'Thanks to the opposition, who thought they had as much right to exercise their lungs in the streets as the ''Salvation Army'', the latter had to cease from their shoutings on Sunday last, the threat by the police to summon disturbers of the peace operating with equal force against them as others. ''Sauce for the goose was sauce for the gander''. The procession, however, paraded the streets and an attempt was made at sensation by the presence of a couple of so-called ''converted roughs'' from Hereford'.

But twenty or so years later, General William Booth was given a great reception when he drove round the streets in an open car on 13 August, 1907. The Salvationists had a hall in Brampton Street but since its destruction by fire in November, 1938, they have had no organisation in the town.

Ross parish church.

ABOVE: The plague cross before its restoration in 1896. LEFT: The cross at the north-east entrance to the churchyard marks the communal grave of the plague victims. The socket stone and shaft are mediaeval, but the cap and cross were added in 1896, the sculptor, A. W. Ursell, working from a sketch of the cross as it was in 1833. RIGHT: This fine piece of marble sculpting is on the tomb of Thomas Westfaling in the parish church. In 1791 Thomas married Mary, the last of the Westfalings, the female line from the Rudhall, and assumed her name.

LEFT: The church soon after the 1952 rebuilding of the top 25 feet of the spire and one of the pinnacles. RIGHT: The trees which up to 100 years ago flourished in Ross Parish Church. BELOW: The interior of the church over 50 years ago.

54

LEFT: In June 1976 the eight bells of the church were taken from the tower for the first time since being cast in 1761, and were taken to Loughborough for tuning and turning. Watching them is Miss Ann Butcher, Secretary of the tower. RIGHT: The 13th century stone coffin near the south porch of the church, not far from where it was discovered. It was empty, but many human bones were found in the vicinity. BELOW: The Bishop of Hereford, the Right Rev John Percival, dedicating the extension to the churchyard in 1909.

When the top 25 feet of the spire was rebuilt in 1952, amateur photographer
John Ashby climbed the 205 feet to the top and took a picture of the town.
The weathercock was refurbished at the same time.

ABOVE: The old Rectory, which was demolished to provide a site for Church Close. On the right in the mid-distance can be seen work starting on the new police station, which was opened in 1958. BELOW: The Anglican Overross Mission Room had a life of nearly 100 years from 1880 until it closed in 1976. This picture was taken by R. E. Davies c1920, when several musicians would accompany the choir and congregation.

Captain William Rhind, founder of the present Evangelical Church in Henry
Street, is depicted preaching at the Market House c1840.

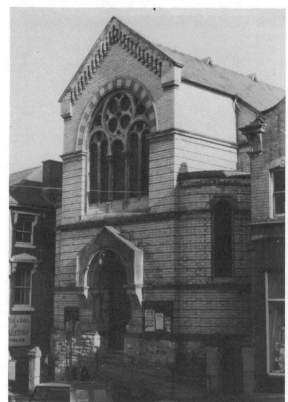
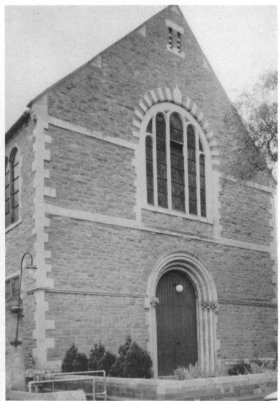

LEFT: The Baptist Church, Broad Street. RIGHT: The Methodist Church, built in 1867 and demolished in 1971. BELOW: The Young Men's Bible Class at the Baptist Church, Broad Street, c1927.

A Swiss Bazaar at Ross Congregational Church c1890. (Photos from County
Library, given by Miss E. Kendall Pearson of Gloucester).

ABOVE: The meeting place of the Society of Friends. INSET: James Cowles Prichard, pioneer anthropologist and one of the founders of the Ethnological Society, was born at Millbrook House, Brookend Street, on 11 February, 1786. The family had lived in Ross for several generations and his father, Thomas Prichard, was a glover, poet and ardent Quaker. BELOW: General William Booth, founder of the Salvation Army, leaving The Graig, Ashfield, home of Henry Southall (in bowler hat) on 13 August, 1907.

61

Ross United Reformed Church. INSET: The Victorian Roman Catholic church in Corpus Christi Lane is now the Kingdom Hall of Jehovah's Witnesses.

ABOVE: The Roman Catholic Church. BELOW: The interior of Ross
Parish Church before the extensive restoration of the 1870s.

ABOVE: Wilton Castle, framed by an arch of Wilton Bridge. BELOW: The pseudo-fortifications of Palace Close.

64

Ross at War

At the point where it overlooks the river, Ross has all the trappings of a fortified town. Turrets cling to a massive wall, battlements surmount buildings and at the best vantage point of all, stands a sturdy tower of the familiar red sandstone, from where one can imagine the sentinels of old looking across the rolling Herefordshire countryside to the distant mountains of Wales. But the imagination would be wrong, for none of these supposed abodes of the warrior has anything to do with war. All are the fruits of the neo-Gothic revival which made a dramatic and not unpleasing transformation of the architecture of this part of the town in the late 1830s.

There is no record of Ross ever having suffered from sacking by the Welsh such as Hereford endured. Maybe protection was given by the men of Archenfield, whose kingdom stretched from the Monnow to the banks of the Wye at Wilton. The *Saxon Chronicle* records, 'In the year 918, a large army sailed from Armorica and advanced towards Archenfield, but being met by the inhabitants and neighbourhood was signally defeated; and again in 1049 some Irish pirates entered the mouth of the Severn, and with the aid of Griffin, King of the Welsh, plundered the country around the Wye'.

The men of Archenfield were among the earliest Christians and were an independent race whom both Saxon and Norman came to terms with rather than attempt to subdue. When fighting the Welsh it was always their privilege and proud boast to be in the vanguard of the attack and the rearguard of retreat, and in the Civil War they were solidly for the King.

Colonel Nicholas Mynne, the local Royalist commander, found Ross impossible to fortify, but made a citadel of the churchyard, using the cliffs on the west, the sunken road on the east (Church Street) and trenches to the north and south.

No attack came, but when Mynne was killed in a skirmish at Redmarley, Colonel Sir Edward Massey occupied Ross for Parliament. He stayed a week, exacting dues from the populace, many of whom found it prudent to declare themselves for Cromwell. On leaving for Hereford, Massey found his way at Wilton Bridge blocked by musketeers from Goodrich Castle, but he quickly overcame them. His horses forded the river and his surprise attack from the rear killed many of the musketeers.

Wilton Castle, reputed to have been built in 1141, was destroyed in the Spring of 1645. Its owner, Sir John Brydges, wanted only to live in peace in a home he regarded more as a manor than a fortress. But after he rejected an ultimatum from his uncle, Sir

John Barnabas, to join the forces of the King, he returned from church one Sunday morning to find his home in flames. He was no longer neutral — he hated the Royalists until he died of smallpox in 1651, still short of his thirtieth birthday.

On the orders of the King, one of the arches of Wilton Bridge was destroyed, but this did not stop Ross experiencing on 3 September of that same year, 1645, the most horrifying night of all its long history. Fourteen thousand Scots had been encircling Hereford for months and when the siege was raised they fled to friendly Gloucestershire. They repaired the bridge to enter Ross and wreak havoc. Even in the next century, when the monarchy had long been restored, old men would recount the ravenous rapacity, haste and hunger of the fleeing army.

In that same week, Ross greeted the King as he paused for refreshment on his way from Monmouth to the relieved Hereford.

In 1646, there was a skirmish at Old Gore when a patrol from Goodrich Castle unsuccessfully tried to ambush Colonel John Birch, who was now commanding the Parliamentarians locally. On 31 July of that year, the conflict around Ross ceased with the surrender of Goodrich Castle after six weeks' bombardment.

In the Napoleonic wars, 600 local men formed into the Archenfield Volunteer Infantry, under the command of Colonel Nourse, of Weston-under-Penyard.

In the Boer War, 21 Ross men were among the 116 Herefordshire and Shropshire volunteers who fought and marched for 12 months in South Africa.

The rifle ranges at Alton Court were now making Ross known among military men, and up to 1914 several regiments held their annual camps at the foot of Penyard, when they enlivened the town with tattoos, band concerts and other social events.

On 5 August 1914, townspeople crowded the Market Place to give B Company of the 1st Herefordshire Regiment a rousing send-off as they left for the First World War. Ninety-eight Ross men gave their lives while serving in the armed forces.

The Second World War brought the sound of enemy arms to Ross for the first time since the Civil War and, strangely, the first bombs to fall in the neighbourhood, on the night of 2 July 1940, made craters at Old Gore, only a few yards from one of the last local engagements of the fraticide nearly three centuries previously.

During the war, 146 high explosive bombs, two oil bombs, and hundreds of incendiaries were dropped in the fields and woods around Ross, but the only one to fall in the town did not explode — which was providential for it was a 500-pounder and it landed in the kitchen garden only 200 ft from the Chase Hotel, the wartime home of 400 girls from Channing School. The bomb fell at 7.30 pm on the night of Thursday 21 November 1940, but its whereabouts were not known until next morning. Nearby houses and the hotel were evacuated until the bomb disposal squad came four days later.

On another night, a plane dived over Ross, releasing a stick of bombs. The first just missed the council houses at Tudorville and the remainder fell along the river bank towards Walford.

Forty-four men from Ross gave their lives in the world-wide conflict.

LEFT: Part of the mock ramparts of 19th century neo-Gothic architecture.
RIGHT: Wilton Castle was burned down by the Royalists in the Civil War.
BELOW: A scene at Wilton Castle, drawn by E. Dayes and engraved by F.
Dukes in 1797. (Courtesy of Hereford City Museums).

INSET: The monument to Colonel William Rudhall in the parish church has the head of Charles I and is dressed as a Roman warrior. He died a bachelor in 1651, the last of the family that had lived at Rudhall since 1306. He is reputed to have demolished one of the arches of Wilton bridge in the Civil War. ABOVE: The men of Ross who volunteered to fight in the South African War in 1900. BELOW: Ross Volunteers on parade before the First World War outside the Drill Hall in Cantilupe Road which later became a magistrates' court.

ABOVE: Ross Volunteers marching down Gloucester Road, c1910.
BELOW: A lighter moment during the First World War: a nurse sings with a
pig in her arms to raise funds for the Red Cross at a Market Place concert.

ABOVE: The first consignment of Fordson tractors to come to the district during the First World War were for the Food Prodution Dept. (Photo: R. E. Davies) BELOW: The choir from the German POW camp in Alton Lane, seen outside the Baptist Church in 1946. INSET: The only bomb to fall in the town did not explode and is now preserved in the grounds of the Chase Hotel, a few yards from where it fell on 21 November, 1940.

To Preserve Prospect

For nearly two centuries the people of Ross neglected the Prospect and let it decay, but when they thought there was a danger that it would be taken away from them they rioted and the outnumbered police deemed it prudent not to interfere.

The story of what are today neat, well-ordered gardens with views commanding the horseshoe bend of the Wye and the wide acres of South Herefordshire stretching to the mountains of Wales, begins, as do so many other Ross stories, with John Kyrle. In October, 1693, he obtained from the owner and Lord of the Manor, Lord Weymouth, a lease for 500 years at a rent of £5 a year, but Weymouth retained the right to raise stone and quarry the land.

Kyrle himself sublet the land for 495 years to William Fisher by lease dated 3 May, 1696. He restricted Fisher to the depasturing of sheep and reserved to himself the right to make walks for the public. But Fisher, who kept the Pounds Inn, next to the Prospect, found the lease too restrictive and, at his request, Kyrle granted him another lease, dated 24 November 1713, allowing him to sublet the land and to depasture pigs. The ground thus degenerated into a piggery and was no longer a pleasant place for recreation.

One hundred years later, the Prospect was being described as 'a mere meadow'. A fountain there had fallen into disuse, the Kyrle arms on the north and south gateways had been destroyed by 'barbarous hands' and soon a brass plate that Kyrle had placed there was ripped away by vandals and thrown into a pool.

In the 1830s, James Barrett bought the Pounds Inn and the pig pens on the land adjoining (the site of the Bishop's palace of mediaeval times) and at a cost of £20,000 erected the Royal Hotel, the hotel tap, coach houses and stables. To do this, he brought Kyrle's and Fisher's leases and, to overcome any question of quarrying, bought the freehold of the Prospect from Lord Weymouth's representatives.

Barrett laid walks and planted flower beds and shrubs, but to prevent constant trespass and damage, he built a wall to enclose the land adjoining the hotel. This led to constant ill-feeling among the townspeople which exploded after his death when the hotel was brought by the Ross Royal Hotel Company. The band of the Rifle Volunteer Corps sought to give twice-weekly concerts on the pleasure grounds and when the people heard that the company had prevented this, trouble started.

On Saturday 10 July, 1869, a crowd trampled on vegetables growing in a plot of ground fenced from the Prospect. The temperature was reaching boiling point and worse was soon to come.

On the following Monday, the very day, coincidentally, that Royal Assent was given to the amendment of the Ross Improvement Act to include the Towns' Police Clauses Act, a mob of 500 invaded the hotel grounds at 6 pm. They trampled on the kitchen gardens, destroyed the ornamental gardens and hacked the wooden billiards room to pieces. They lit a bonfire and fed it with doors, gates and posts, shrubs and hedges. Hour after hour the destruction went on, and it was long after midnight when a sharp shower dampened the blaze and sent the rioters home.

The town had only five constables and they did not interfere, but at dawn came reinforcements from Hereford, under the command of the Chief Constable, Captain James Drummond Telfer; armed with cutlasses, they guarded the hotel for the next 24 hours.

Twelve men — a dyer, a mason, a cabinet maker, a porter, a plumber, a coach builder, a wheelwright, three tailors and two labourers — were brought before the magistrates, charged with causing a riot. Three were discharged and the other nine were committed to the Assizes where they were accorded the moderate penalty of being bound over to keep the peace.

The local antagonism towards the Royal was quelled when Thomas Blake, a dominant figure in 19th century Ross, the hotel company's first secretary and later its chairman, bought the freehold of the best and largest portion of the Prospect and presented it to Ross by deed for the use of the town for ever.

Blake's gift was kept anonymous for two years, his solicitor, John Skyrme, simply telling the Town Commissioners at their meeting on 7 June, 1870 that the Chancery and other proceedings relative to the Prospect and the public rights and the Royal Hotel Company had been settled. It was proposed to convey to the Town Commissioners what was called the outer Prospect free of expense, save the approval of the draft by their solicitor, provided they agreed to take the conveyance and would keep the ground in order. The Commissioners accepted the offer and considered that £5 a year would be enough to keep the ground in good order!

ABOVE: William Farrer's impression of Ross Church from the Prospect in 1832. (Courtesy of Hereford City Museums). BELOW: Gateways to the Prospect.

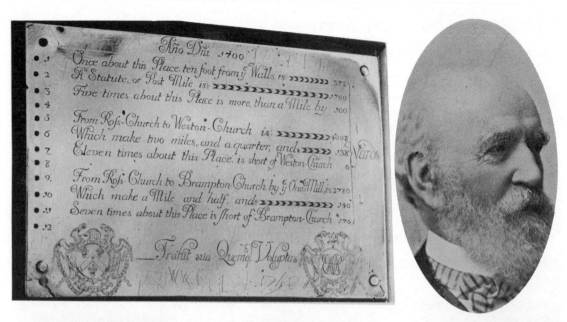

LEFT: The brass plate put by Kyrle in the north wall at the west corner of the Prospect was torn down by vandals and lay hidden for years in a pond; the plate, measuring 12 ins by 8 ins, is now in the Town Council Chamber. RIGHT: Thomas Blake, 1825-1901, was a dominant figure in 19th century Ross. After the 1869 riots he secured most of the Prospect to the ownership of the town for ever. BELOW: A plaque in the foyer of the Royal Hotel.

Royal Victoria School

On Boxing Day morning, as the world springs to life again after the languor of Christmas Day, cars stream out of town along the Hereford road to the Ross Harriers meeting at Harewood End. Along the same road in the early years of Victoria's reign, would have been seen on Boxing Day some twenty boys marching briskly the eight miles to the home of the Member of Parliament, Mr K. Hoskins, of Birch House, Much Birch. They were the monitors and senior pupils from the Royal Ross and Archenfield British and Foreign School, which descends from Wilton Road to Wye Street, the building that now houses a Masonic temple. Mr Hoskins was their benefactor and he had invited them to dinner.

The boys had been warned by their master, Captain George Adams, that if they neglected to have their hair cut or if they had the least speck on their white duck pinafore uniform, they would be sent home. With black leather belt and blue cloth cap completing their uniform, the boys were immaculate as they lined up for Captain Adams' inspection before setting out on their three-hour march. At Birch House they were given a dinner of roast beef and plum pudding, with a glass of wine and they sang hymns and received a shilling each from Mrs Hoskins before starting their march back to Ross.

The boys were well accustomed to having little leisure. The summer holidays lasted just a week, the Christmas holidays from 14 December to 4 January and on Easter Monday they attended school for the half-yearly examination. If they did well, they were rewarded with cakes.

It was in 1834 that Captain Adams and Mr W.R. Hall addressed the people of Ross in the following terms. 'The deplorable state of public morals as evinced on the Sabbath Day, particularly in the streets at night and in the Market House by juvenile delinquents prove that the present public schools are inadequate to check the prevailing of all evil. They therefore call upon the friends of social order to aid them with their suport in the arduous undertaking in which they are engaged, namely to establish a school open to all sects and parties where a religious education shall be given, such as will afford the children the means of becoming respectable and happy in this life, with prospects of a blissful immortality in that which is to come'.

The Church of England clergy were not impressed. The Rector, Canon Thomas Underwood, wrote withholding his support because the British and Foreign School Society rejected the creeds and Catechism of the Established Church. Captain Adams was not easily dissuaded. He wrote to the MP who invited him to breakfast at Birch House. Whether Captain Adams had to walk there is not recorded, but Mr Hoskins declared himself most friendly to the undertaking and gave a donation of £25 and a loan of £100 free of interest for two years. He also obtained a Government grant of £100.

In 1835, a public meeting in the town welcomed the plan on account of its liberal principle, its great simplicity and economy, and decided that the children of 'small farmers, little tradesmen, mechanics and labourers' residing in the town and neighbourhood were proper objects of the institution. A committee was elected with Thomas Prichard, banker, as its chairman and including the Baptist minister, the Rev Edward Claypole.

There were difficulties in finding a site, which Captain Adams attributed to the secret persecution and opposition of the clergy of the Established Church, but Mrs Ann Tristram solved the problem by offering the committee a piece of land, measuring 50ft by 33ft, which they purchased for £60. The boys' school opened on 19 September, 1837, with 50 on the roll, children of labourers and artisans paying twopence a week for their education.

Within a year, the Established Church's opposition was on the wane, for the Bishop of Hereford, Thomas Musgrave, visited the school, accompanied by the Archdeacon and other clergy. The Bishop was invited to question the boys on their knowledge of the Bible but he declined and requested the Archdeacon to do so. Captain Adams wrote in his log: 'The Archdeacon continued a considerable time in the examination, much to the satisfaction of all who heard them, though the manner in which they were questioned was quite different from that to which they have been accustomed'.

In 1840, the school was extended to provide for the education of girls, but it did not survive the century.

The Church of England had its own school in the town — the Walter Scott School, in a building that continues to dominate Old Gloucester Road. It was set up as a Blue Coat School in 1709 by Dr Charles Whiting, Rector, the Viscount Scudamore, and others 'for the instruction and education of poor boys and girls of the parish of Ross in the Christian religion, according to the usages of the Church of England as by law established, and for the clothing and otherwise assisting of such poor boys and girls as far as the means of such school should extend'. The children of poor tradesmen and 'other industrious persons not being burthensome to the parish' were to have preference.

An early pupil of the school was Walter Scott, (no relation to the novelist), the son of John Scott, carpenter. At the age of 13 he ran away to London, so the story goes, afraid that he would be hanged if it were discovered that he had stolen pears from a local garden. He learnt the trade of plasterer from his uncle, amassed a fortune and became a Citizen of London. Returning to his native town at the age of 69, he was distressed to find his old school falling into decay, and wrote to the treasurer, 'As I have no children and as God has blest me with a small fortune, I have a mind to reestablish the Blue Coat Charity School in Ross, as I had the little learning I have there'.

Scott died the next year and by his will, dated 2 December 1785, he gave the annual sum of £200 towards the support of a school at Ross, at the discretion of his executors. An information was filed in the Court of Chancery for the purpose of establishing and regulating his charity; by an order dated 25 January 1793, it was decreed that the same should be established, and it was referred to the Master to approve a scheme to carry it into effect. It was determined by the court that the school which was the object of the testator's bounty was the Blue Coat School, and the scheme provided that it should be called Walter Scott's Charity School. By a deed of 23 August, 1798, a school house erected by Scott's executors and a sum of £6,666 13s 4d New South Sea Annuities, which they had set apart to answer his charitable donation of £200 a year, were secured to the scheme's trustees.

Thirty boys and thirty girls, from six to thirteen years of age, were taught at the school, but to meet rising costs with an almost static income, the numbers were reduced in an effort to keep the school open. The economic pressures were too great and in 1928 the school had to close, but money from the endowment continues to help the boys and girls of Ross to buy tools, books and equipment for apprenticeships and further education.

An even older school was in the churchyard on the site of the present St Mary's Hall. A Latin grammar school was founded there in the 16th century in the reign of Edward VI, but it fell into ruins. It was re-endowed by Lord of the Manor, Lord Weymouth, in 1709 with a rent charge of £10, payable out of his manors of Weobley and Ross. Again, the building became derelict and in 1806 was replaced a second time. It now became a National school, named St Mary's and 60 boys were taught in one large room and 50 girls in another, their ages ranging from six to thirteen years. The school was under the management of two presidents, the Lord of the Manor and the Rector, and six governors.

Other schools to be found in Ross immediately prior to the 1870 Act were Madame du Beau's school for young ladies at Clairville House, Mr Thomas's establishment for young gentlemen at Palmerston House, an infants' school in Old Gloucester Road, and the Ross Academy for Boys in Dock Street (Wye Street).

The school at Palmerston House survived until the Second World War; Clairville House became the first home of Ross Conservative Club in 1885, but later resumed its educational role as the privately-owned Ross High School until it closed in 1958 on the retirement of its principal, Miss M. S. Morling. Most of the other schools went out of existence with the opening of the board schools in Cantilupe Road in 1874. They were built at a cost of £6,137 to accommodate 420 children, and several generations of boys and girls spent all their school days there.

In the 1930s the need for a central school (midway between elementary and grammar school education) was realised, but the outbreak of war in 1939 brought the embryo scheme to a halt. By the end of the war, the Education Act of 1944 providing secondary education for all and the rising of the school leaving age to 15 had made the demand for extra accommodation acute. Lessons were being held in buildings scattered all over the town, church halls and temporary accomodation being pressed into service as additional classrooms.

In 1953, Herefordshire's first new secondary modern school was opened at Overross. It had been built at a cost of £122,250, a million bricks were used, and a bonus for the community at large was the biggest and best hall Ross had ever known. The town now also possessed a school giving a broader education to its children and to those from the district who would otherwise have spent all their school days in the villages. The price to be paid was the adverse effect on country life when it was found in several instances that there were now too few pupils to warrant the village school remaining open.

With the transfer of the children of eleven years and over, the primary school took over the entire premises in Cantilupe Road, but even this was insufficient for the increasing numbers of children and the wider educational facilities required. Classrooms at the old Walter Scott School were brought into use but in the end it was not lack of room that closed the school, but the danger to life and limb.

Managers and staff became increasingly worried as the 95-year-old red sandstone crumbled ominously and stones were dislodged. County Council architects were called in and they in turn brought Ministry of Education architects to Ross. When none of them could guarantee the safety of the building, the special executive committee of the Herefordshire Education Committee ordered the immediate closing of the school during the 1968 Easter holidays. After a delayed start to the summer term, the children found they were to have lessons in classrooms provided by other schools and church halls in the town; some forms had to make the 14 mile journey daily to Hereford to use classrooms in city schools.

Within six weeks, the Ministry of Education had given consent for a new school, and though a start was soon made with the building it was two years before all the classes were back together again with the opening of the £137,434 Ashfield Park School in 1970.

In 1976, an annexe to the primary school came into use at Northside, Brampton Road. It had been erected for classes of sub-normal children, but happily, the paucity of these cases made the accomodation redundant before it was ever used and the four classrooms were turned over to the teaching of infants living in the north of the town.

The Convent School, opened in 1934, found it more and more difficult to keep alive in the gathering inflation but fortunately it did not suffer the fate of Walter Scott School, for in 1975 the State took over much of the financial burden. Fees had risen to £35 a term but these disappeared overnight with the opening of the St Joseph's Roman Catholic Voluntary Aided School in buildings in the Convent grounds erected at a cost of over £70,000. The school had places for 120 children between the ages of five and eleven years and all but two of these were filled on the first day of the new arrangement.

The red brick Ross Grammar School came into being as a result of the Education Act giving Education Authorities powers to establish secondary schools. It was 1912 before the school was opened, having been built at a cost of £6,000, the County Council finding £3,600 and the Urban Council making a twopenny rate to raise the other £2,400. Ross Rural Council refused invitations to contribute, one councillor saying when after 18 months they were again asked to help, 'The urban council have a white elephant and they want to sell it to us'.

The school had places for 100 pupils when it opened and there were 20 girls and 19 boys attending on its first day. A quarter of the places were free and the others were at £2 a term, except for a solitary boarder whose parents paid ten guineas a term for him to lodge at the headmaster's home through the week. With the 1944 Education Act giving secondary education for all, the school fees, which had risen to £4 4s, were abolished.

With the Grammar School and Overross School meeting the needs of children over a wide range of age, aptitude and ability, all seemed set fair for undisturbed decades of useful work, but in the autumn of 1979 the 400 children at the Grammar School and 800 at Overross were merged into one comprehensive school named the John Kyrle High School.

INSET: An early declaration from Clairville School, Ross. BELOW: The Walter Scott School, now the salerooms of an auctioneer.

ABSTRACT

OF THE

CONVEYANCE AND DEED OF TRUST,

FOR ESTABLISHING

WALTER SCOTT'S

CHARITY SCHOOL,

IN THE PARISH OF ROSS,

IN THE COUNTY OF HEREFORD,

Dated 28th August, 1798.

WALTER SCOTT DIED IN LONDON, 4TH 12TH MONTH, 1786, AGED 70.

Printed by order of the Trustees and Governors ; and Reprinted by an order of the Governors, 2nd of 9th month, September, 1822, with the additional Rules and Regulations of the 12th of 8th month August, 1822 ; and is most respectfully presented to the children of the said school, by their friend

NATHANIEL MORGAN.

4th month, April, 1823.

TO THE ABOVE IS SUBJOINED A COPY OF THE WILL AND A SHORT ACCOUNT OF JAMES BAKER, ANOTHER GREAT BENEFACTOR TO THIS PARISH, WHO DIED IN LONDON, 24TH 6TH MONTH, 1836, AGED 72.

LEFT: The foundation of Walter Scott's charity school. RIGHT: The tomb of Walter Scott who went from Ross to London and made a fortune, much of which he bequeathed to the benefit of the town's Bluecoat School. BELOW: Ross Grammar School's production of 'Bardell v Pickwick' in 1923.

LEFT: The British and Foreign School in Wye Street. RIGHT: The council schools in Cantilupe Road, built in 1874 and demolished in 1968. CENTRE and BELOW: In August, 1979, three weeks after the Grammar School closed to be replaced by John Kyrle High School, the roof was badly damaged by fire.

ABOVE: An artist's impression of John Kyrle dispensing aid to the needy.
BELOW: The 16th century Rudhall almshouses in Church Street.

82

Men of Charity

Almshouses in several parts of the town keep alive the names of men of charity. Webbe's almshouses in Copse Cross Street were provided by the £800 bequeathed by Thomas Webbe, carpenter, of Mouncton, Llanwarne, by his will proved on 2 December 1614.

Perrock's Hospital in Old Gloucester Road was founded in 1510 by Richard Worcester and came into the possession of the Church of Ross. After its alienation it descended to Charles Perrock of Ross, a mercer, who in 1605 settled it on the vicar, churchwardens, and overseers of the poor in trust for four parishioners. A report by HM Inspector, William Good, in 1866, described it as a small worn-out building, not fit for habitation, but still occupied by one man and three women. It was rebuilt in 1889 by Thomas Blake.

The Rev William Pye, in 1615, settled on the same officials an almshouse in Edde Cross Street and this was exchanged in 1792 for another building in the same street. In 1854, Thomas Roberts, of London, repaired it and endowed it with £1,500 Consols.

In 1654 Phillip Markye gave an almshouse in Trenchar Street (as the lower part of Edde Cross Street was called) for the use of six poor widows. This too was restored by Thomas Blake and was subsequently sold to Ross Urban Council.

The best-known almshouses are those in Church Street with their unusually attractive Tudor gabled dormers. They are on the site of a hospice founded in the 14th century and which was part of the lands and tenements belonging to a chantry suppressed during the Reformation. In 1575, William Rudhall repaired the hospital and vested it in his heirs for the poor.

The most munificent charity of all is that of James Baker, who was born in Ross and was a nailor by trade, but subsequently went to London where he made a fortune as an ironmonger and marine store dealer. By his will, proved on 11 July, 1836, he bequeathed the residue of his estate for the benefit of the poor of Ross and after the death of his widow in 1850 the Court of Chancery established a scheme by which £16,666 13s 4d Consols was carried over in trust.

In 1957, the Charity Commissioners instituted a scheme for the amalgamation of all these charities and 14 small bread charities to be administered by the Ross Charity Trustees. The income from the investments is now devoted to the modernisation and maintenance of the almshouses.

ABOVE:Webbe's almshouses with their modern accoutrements. BELOW:
The Larruperz raising money at Ross Hospital Carnival, May 1928.

ABOVE: A woeful pair of twins photographed by Richard Davies in Brampton Street earlier this century.

BELOW: Miss Mary Sarah Hall, born 17 January, 1827, died on 7 March, 1932, holds the town's record for longevity. She sang in the parish church choir in her youth and later gave the organ chamber in the parish church.

ABOVE: Ross Harriers meeting on the Swan corner in 1919. LEFT: George Richards, known as 'Rumsher', was a regular runner with local hunts. Local people backed him against a professional in a race to Hope Mansel and back, which Rumsher won. When he died in 1927 the hunting fraternity had a 'whip round' to meet the funeral expenses. (Photo: H. E. Wilkins) RIGHT: One of the oldest extant cups competed for by Ross farmers, won in 1866 by Edwin Jones of Pencoyd for growing the best four acres of turnips within ten miles of Ross, using the special manure supplied by H. Webb.

Recreation

From Liverpool and Nottingham, from Bristol and London, from the cities of Oxford and Cambridge and from 50 other places, rowing men converged on Ross on August Bank Holiday, 1975. It is a similar story every year, for the regatta has put the town on the rowing map of a large slice of England and Wales.

Regattas have been held at Ross ever since the first August Bank Holiday in 1874. Then, there were races for coracles and canoes, young daredevils walked a greasy pole, and the day ended with a fireworks spectacular. Now the regattas are much more sophisticated, with races every three minutes from 10 am to 7.30 pm as the eights, fours, pairs and scullers battle for the trophies.

Fishing the river has of course been a means of livelihood and a sport since man came to the valley. In 1827, T. B. Watkins wrote that the Wye was celebrated for its salmon, which was formerly in great abundance at Ross, but owing to the obstruction of the New Weir (at Whitchurch) it had become scarce. But pike, grayling, trout, perch, gudgeon, dace, roach and chub were plentiful.

At the beginning of the last century, a race meeting was held at Broad Meadow every August and in the 1920s an attempt was made to establish Weirend as a racecourse, but the project did not survive more than two or three meetings. On the other hand, Ross Harriers, founded in 1821, are still flourishing.

The cricket club's history stretches back to 1837 when it staged a match between Married Men and Single Men at Weirend; the marrieds won by seven wickets. In 1851, 22 of Ross played an all-England eleven, including Wisden and Clarke in their bowlers. In the three-day match, six Ross wickets fell without a run and all 22 could muster only 53 runs. England made 130 and Ross were all out for 69 in the second innings to be beaten by an innings and eight runs.

Another memorable match was in 1871 when the immortal W. G. Grace and his brother G. F. Grace were in the Ross team that met the neighbouring village of Weston-under-Penyard. Ross scored 311, of which W.G. hit 95 and his brother 174. W.G. took all the Weston wickets to dismiss them for 56.

While Europe was descending into war in the opening days of August 1914, Ross was playing the MCC at the Park. MCC included three county professionals: Wainwright of Yorkshire, Alleton, the giant hitter from Nottinghamshire, and Newman from Wiltshire. Ross was beaten by six wickets.

The golf club was founded in 1903 and for 22 years used a nine-hole course at Alton

Court where two of the tee shots had the handicap of crossing the Ross-Monmouth railway line. In 1925 the club moved to a nine-hole course at Rudhall and nearly 40 years later carved a fine eighteen-hole course out of the woodland near the motorway at Jays Green.

Many are the Association Football clubs that have been born and faded away, but none has gained honours beyond those of the county league of Herefordshire and Gloucestershire. Talbot's Meadow is the traditional home of Ross soccer, but since 1963 clubs have also been using the pitches at Ross Sports Centre where a voluntary organisation, representative of several local clubs, levelled and re-seeded land held on lease by the urban council.

Ross Rugby Club dates back to the 1870s and on 13 March 1879, outstripped many top clubs of today by 70 years or more by playing a match under floodlight. Three 8,000 candle-power lamps connected to a Siemens generator provided the light for a match at the Marsh against Newent which Ross won by a goal and six tries to a disputed goal.

On its formation at Ross in 1908, South Herefordshire Lawn Tennis Club had 300 members and until 1939 held open tournaments that attracted players of nationwide repute.

South Herefordshire Foxhounds, the hockey, cycling and rifle clubs all were founded in the last century, and in more recent years the bowling and motor sports clubs have become popular.

Swimming has become a sport for all only within the last 20 years. In July, 1878, George Webb celebrated his 20th birthday by swimming the four miles from Foy Bridge to Wilton Bridge in 1 hour 37 minutes. But the river with its currents and tangled reeds is no place for the inexperienced and in nearly every heat wave the Wye claims at least one victim.

It was suggested that the Silver Jubilee of King George V in 1935 should be commemorated by the provision of a pool, but the scheme was abandoned. In the 1950s, enthusiasts again began to explore the possibilities and an association was formed. After seven years they had £4,000 in the kitty but even the most optimistic had to concede that no real progress had been made, for costs were rising much more rapidly than funds could be raised. In 1969, the association handed the project over to a joint committee of Ross Urban Council and Ross and Whitchurch Rural Council, who were immediately confronted with ministerial refusal to sanction a loan. All seemed hopeless until suddenly, early in 1971, the Department of the Environment informed the councils that the money was available, provided work started before 31 March, the end of the financial year, After being thwarted for so long, the councils were suddenly given no more than 11 weeks to put the plan into action. But they were not to be caught out, for they had long had everything ready for the green light. So on 3 March, Bernard Hackett, who had guided the scheme for many years, turned the first sod for the construction and 30 months later opened the pool, built to county and district championship standards at a cost of £170,000.

Not only in the realm of sport do country folk delight in pitting their skills against one another. Ross had its own agricultural show in 1867 with classes for sheep and pigs, grain and roots. It did not survive, unlike Harewood End Agricultural Society, which has held a show in the district every year since 1891, with the exception of the war years.

Herefordshire Agricultural Society, forerunner of the Three Counties, held its show at the Marsh Meadow in 1887, and in 1904 the Two Counties Show, as it had now become with the amalgamation with Worcester, was held at Ashfield. On both occasions, the town was en fête, as it has been much more recently in 1959, 1967 and 1974 when the national ploughing championships were held in the district. For each of these, an ox has been roasted at the Market Place, though on the last occasion something went wrong with the cooking and the carcase was declared inedible.

Ross Fruit and Flower Society held its first meeting in 1825, and various societies put on shows at intervals until 1935 since when Ross Horticultural Society has staged a show nearly every year.

Among other organisations that existed in the town early in the 19th century were the Institution for the Encouragement and Benefit of Faithful Female Servents and a Society for the Prosecution of Felons. Ross also had a library in 1817 and two reading societies.

From its opening in 1862 until its destruction by fire in 1939, the first floor of the Corn Exchange was the centre of indoor entertainment. The Great Chevalier and the D'Oyly Carte Opera Company were among household names to perform in the hall above the market. In 1922, the hall was licensed as a cinema, taking the name of the New Theatre, and there Ross Operatic and Dramatic Society performed the light operas that were a feature of social life between the wars. From there in 1931, Ross Orpheus Society, a male voice choir, made one of the first ever broadcasts from Herefordshire.

The town's first cinema was The Kyrle, built in Gloucester Road in 1913 and closed in 1950. The Roxy Cinema was opened two months after fire destroyed the New Theatre.

Choral singing has long been popular among this community on the edge of Wales and the town has had several choirs, some still in existence. Ross Orchestral Society, formed in 1915, presents an annual concert and Ross Town Band had a life of half a century from its formation in 1924.

Summer carnivals have been held at infrequent intervals, and each year since 1956 the town has had its Christmas Carnival. The merriest occasion of the year is when Santa rides through packed streets to the Market House in a spectacular float, preceded by Scouts with flaming torches. He is welcomed by the civic heads before the free distribution of 2,400 packages to the eager children.

ABOVE: Ross Orpheus Society, led by F. J. Parsons, c1927. BELOW: Col John Maclean, Lord Lieutenant of Herefordshire and President of Ross Golf Club, inaugurates with a straight drive the first nine holes of the club's new course at Jay's Green in 1964.

90

ABOVE: Ross at play at the town's swimming pool. BELOW: The
Women's Institute keeping alive traditional country dances at nearby
Bridstow.

91

Nous, par cette Charte, décidons que nos deux villes feront tout pour s'unir désormais dans un commun effort en vue développer les rapports entre nos deux populations, d'encourager l'étude des langues et cultures Françaises et Anglaises, de promouvoir des liens étroits entre nos écoles et associations Françaises et Anglaises, et d'assurer une base solide à l'amitié des personnes, comme contribution concrète à l'entente internationale.

En foi de quoi nous signons ce quatorze Octobre MCMXXIII.

Le Maire de Condé-sur-Noireau

Le Président du Comité de Jumelage de Condé-sur-Noireau

We hereby resolve that our two Towns shall henceforth join together in a common endeavour to improve communication between our people, to encourage the study of the French and English languages and cultures, to foster close ties between our English and French schools and societies and to provide a sound basis for personal friendships as a practical contribution to International Understanding.

As Witness our hands ...

This fourteenth day of October MCMXXIII.

The Mayor of Ross-on-Wye.

Chairman of Ross-on-Wye - Condé-sur-Noireau Twinning Association.

In 1978 Ross was twinned with the town of Condé-sur-Noireau, Normandy. The charter (LEFT) was signed at the top of the Market House steps, before a large crowd. RIGHT: Kenneth Riches, Mayor of Ross, is seen signing the charter, accompanied by the Mayor of Condé, Maurice Piart.

In 1960 the town centre was transformed when the George Hotel and several other buildings were demolished to make way for the 11 shops at George Place.

ABOVE: Robert Pashley died in 1956 at the age of 76. In 50 years on the Wye he landed 10,237 salmon, 29 over 40lb. His best year was 1936, when he caught 678, weighing 10,822lb. (Photo: *The Field*) BELOW: Ross Rowing Club (foreground) finishing astern of Bewdley at Ross Regatta, 1978. (Photo: O. Ward)

94

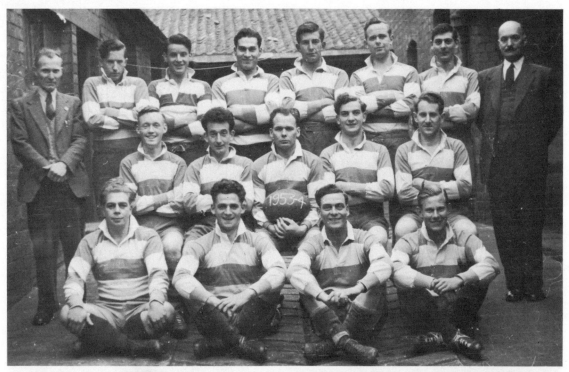

ABOVE: Ross Rugby Club, 1953-54. (Photo: T. W. Passey) BELOW: The club house of Ross Rowing Club, opened in 1978.

ABOVE: Ross United Services won a galaxy of trophies in the 1951-52 season. (Photo: Donovan C. Wilson) BELOW: Ross Cricket Club First Eleven, c1950.

ABOVE: A gathering of the National Home Reading Union at Ross, c1903.
BELOW: Officers of the 'Man of Ross' Lodge of Oddfellows, 1914-18.

ROSS

"Man of Ross" Lodge of Oddfellows, M.U.; Court "Man of Ross, No. 3,344, A.O.F.;" "Man of Ross" Lodge, A.O.S., A.U.

A GRAND

FETE

AND GALA,

IN CONNECTION WITH THE ABOVE SOCIETIES, WILL BE HELD ON

WHIT·MONDAY

NEXT, MAY 30th, 1898.

THERE WILL BE

A Combined Procession

Of the Members at 11.30 a.m., starting from the Town Hall, headed by the BAND of the 1st H.R.V. (B Company)—by the kind permission of the Officers—proceeding to a Field near the Cattle Market, where

A LUNCHEON

WILL BE PROVIDED AT 12.30.

ABOVE: and RIGHT: Poster for Ross Fete, 30 May, 1898.

98

100 Yards Handicap Flat Race (open to Boys over 12 Years of age, who are Members of the Juvenile Societies, or Sons of Members of the adult Lodges). First Prize, 10s.; Second Prize, 2s. 6d.; Third Prize, 1s.

80 Yards Handicap Flat Race (for Boys under 12 Years of age, and open as above). First Prize, 10s.; Second Prize, 2s. 6d.

Tug of War (10 a Side. Competing Teams to find their own Ropes). Prize, £2 10s. Entrance Fee, 2s. 6d. each Team.

Entries, with Entrance Fees, to be made not later than Tuesday, May 24th, to T. WATKINS, 19, Broad Street, Ross. —

GRAND

Comic Football Match

BETWEEN TWO WELL-KNOWN TEAMS, IN GROTESQUE COSTUME.

Marvellous & ACROBATIC VARIETY

ENTERTAINMENTS

The Committee have arranged with **Mr. TOM WOOD**, of Upper Easton, Bristol, the Premier Fete and Gala Caterer and Firework Agent, to provide an attractive and varied Programme of Stage Performances, for which he has secured the services of the following well-known Artistes of London and Continental fame, forming one of the best Entertainments ever witnessed in the Provinces, who will give **AFTERNOON and EVENING PERFORMANCES.**

Grand Starring Engagement of the Renowned Acrobats and Double Trapeze Performers,

LETTO and AL'HO,

In their UNEQUALLED VARIETY GYMNASTIC PERFORMANCE.

Two of the cleverest and most daring Artistes travelling. The World-famed Athletes in new and original Gymnastic Achievements. Grand Performance, up-to-date, introducing sensational Single and Double Somersaults. A most wonderful Gymnastic Display. Splendid Dresses and Stage Appointments.

COSTLY Engagement of MARTO, the Man Frog, Contortionist, &c.

Very Costly Engagement of Miss HETTY VANDEAN, the Dashing Serio-Comic and Dancer.

Important Engagement of the DUBLIN DAISIES,
The Hibernian LAUGHTER MERCHANTS. The greatest Knockabout Artistes of the day.

Special Engagement of Prof. FAY, the World-renowned Ventriloquist, with his Wooden-Headed Family.

Very Costly Engagement and First Appearance of HERR IZAL, the Royal Illusionist.

Engagement of another Big Turn, Buchanan & Tower, Negro Comedians, Vocalists, and Sketch Artistes.

Special Important Engagement of Mr. HARRY MOTRAMOS, the London Star Vocal Character Comedian.
PIANIST - - - - - MR. FREDERICK FEY.

The BAND will play for DANCING on the Field.
All kinds of REFRESHMENTS at Moderate Charges.

Admission, SIXPENCE. Children under 12, Half Price.

Stratford and Trotter, Printers, "Gazette" Office, High Street, Ross.

1907.   1907.

Ross Regatta.

BANK HOLIDAY,

MONDAY, AUGUST 5th.

On the Benhall Course, Ross-on-Wye.

COMMENCES AT 1 P.M.

Admission and Ferry - · - · - One Shilling.

Official Programme, Price 2d.

STRATFORD AND TROTTER, PRINTERS, "GAZETTE" OFFICE, ROSS.

Final part of the programme for the Ross Regatta, Monday 5 August, 1907.

Daily Bread

From the beginning, Ross has always served the farmland that surrounds it. A mill stands on the Rudhall brook today, as one did when William of Normandy's armies came.

The present mill at Brookend was built in 1893 and until the 1950s water from the brook drove its turbines. It has not been used for the production of flour since a fire in 1947, but the South Herefordshire Agricultural Co-operative Society Ltd who operate it, mill 11,000-12,000 tons of cereals a year, nearly all from neighbouring farms; this is mixed with proteins, soya beans, fish meal and other ingredients to make balanced rations for all classes of livestock.

Through the ages, the craftsmanship of Ross men — smiths, wheelwrights, coopers and many others — was usually devoted to the needs of those living in and around the town, but as early as the 16th century, Ross had a provincial reputation for the quality of its boots. In 1576, Lord Talbot of Goodrich Castle, sent 'a payre of Ross bootes' to his father. As late as 1867, there were 16 boot and shoemakers in business.

The Roman iron works at Ariconium have had their successors. In the 17th century Camden described Ross as famous for its smiths and in 1760 John Partridge brought upwards of 100 skilled workmen from Harborne, near Birmingham, and established them in New Street in a long row of nail shops. In the last century Kell Brothers had an extensive foundry and agricultural machine manufactory at the Brookend and about 1870 Perkins and Bellamy opened their iron works in Broad Street and the Crofts, employing 70 men and boys in the production of agricultural and household goods. This firm had their own electric light plant, but public supply did not become available until 1902 when the Ross Electric Light and Power Company built their station at the Brookend. Electricity was generated there for about 30 years until the company became absorbed by the Shropshire, Worcestershire and Staffordshire Electric Company.

The Rope Walk recalled the days when the manufacture of rope required a long stretch, and Tankyard Lane gains its name from the extensive tannery established there by Smyth and Co in 1837.

In 1842, Joseph Turnock came to Ross from Staffordshire to make his home at Merrivale where he invented the Merrivale grate, described as an ingenious device producing maximum warmth with a minimum of fuel. In his obituary 50 years later, it

101

was written, 'Thousands of these grates are in existence and will perpetuate the name of Joseph Turnock for many years to come'.

Turnock made an even greater impact by developing the Alton Court Brewery in Station Street. Until its closure in 1956, following the takeover by the Stroud Brewery, it was one of the biggest employers of labour, besides providing a large area with liquid sustenance!

The closure came at a time when the unemployment situation in the town was becoming serious. The drift from the land, the run down at the end of the war of the munitions factory at Hereford and the aircraft factories at Gloucester, and the closure of the oil refinery and other industries that had been brought to Ross as a haven from the bombers, all meant fewer and fewer jobs. Many were forced to travel out of town daily to the cable works at Lydbrook which itself closed in 1965, or to the rapidly-expanding Ranks plant at Mitcheldean.

Some industry did keep going, like the laundry which since 1899 has consistently provided employment for about 50, nearly all women, and when the clouds threatening mass unemployment were at their blackest, they began to clear. For several years the urban council had been trying to persuade industry to come to the Camp Meadow estate where the steel Nissen huts erected at the start of the Second World War had been used successively by the military, prisoners of war, displaced persons from Europe and finally Ross people themselves, squatters who could find no other home.

At last, in 1956, the council's efforts and patience were rewarded. Tom Shepherd, whose father had been a doctor in the town, returned to form the Haigh Engineering Company and open up a factory for the manufacture of waste disposal systems of his own design. Mr Shepherd died in 1975 but the factory continues in the family ownership with an employment roll of 160 and a market in 55 countries.

On land adjoining, came in 1959 the German company of Wolf Tools, who built impressive buildings for the promotion of their garden tools, and in 1961 came what has grown into the biggest factory of all, the Woodville Rubber Company, who by 1979 had 625 on the employment roll, the equivalent of ten per cent of the entire population of the town.

The factory was bought by Eddie Brewster and William Hodson who had founded the company in 1948 at Woodville, near Burton-on-Trent, and which was now desperately needing land for expansion. In 1967 they sold out to an American company, Garlock Incorporated, and it now belongs to Colt Industries of Park Avenue, New York. Ten acres of the 13½ acre site have been developed for the production of advanced technological precision mouldings, with 40 per cent of its sale overseas. On 1 June 1979, the company's name was changed to Woodville Polymer Engineering, to emphasise its engineering and polymer aspects, only a small percentage of rubber now being used.

A variety of industry has been brought by an influx over the last ten years of several small factories to a corner of the Alton Road estate and the old railway station. The latter lay derelict for ten years after the last trains ran, but has been transformed since South Herefordshire District Council sought the aid of the Development Commission working with the Council for Small Industries in Rural Areas. The site has been renamed the Ashburton Industrial Estate and when Lord Northfield, Chairman of the Development Commission, officially opened it in 1979, the first stage, covering two acres for six factory units, was well under way. Lord Northfield said the Commission was acquiring a further five and a half acres and was hoping to build 10,000 square feet of factory space in each of the next five years.

ABOVE: An 1896 picture of the coopers at Lugg and Son's, Broad Street.
BELOW: A festive 19th century scene outside James Woolf's furniture removal business in Gloucester Road.

LEFT: A tree grew from the chimney of this disused factory, once occupied by Perkins and Bellamy and used in the First World War for making jam. ABOVE: A stone bottle made in Ross in the year before Waterloo. BELOW: One of the earliest cars to be seen in Ross was this Peiper, photographed in Gloucester Road. At the wheel is William Butcher, with his sons, Jack and Alan, in the back.

CENTRE: Toothpaste was made at The Man of Ross House early this
century. ABOVE: Mr Butcher and son Alan at Brookend Street Post Office
in the late 19th century. BELOW: For centuries Ross was well-known for its
boots. This picture from Milward's shows rolls of leather about to be taken
from the railway station.

ABOVE: Ross Market House in the early 20th century, and BELOW:
beneath the arches, c1900.

ABOVE: The Market House clock tower under repair in 1955. BELOW:
The market of the 1970s.

'The present day market — a far cry from Bishop de Bethune's market of
more than 800 years ago.

ABOVE: A mill has been at or near this site in the Brookend since Saxon times. BELOW: On 19 September, 1974, farmers throughout the EEC demonstrated to draw attention to the perilous state of their industry. At 11 am farm tractors converged on the George Cross.

ABOVE: The weir of One Mill as it was before alteration in 1962. It possibly gets it name from being the first mill at Ross, mentioned in Domesday.
BELOW: The withy beds of the Wye provided the raw material for the local basket-making industry which survived until the mid-20th century. (Photo: H. E. Wilkins)

110

ROSS.

Unreserved Sale of Building Material.

WALTER MORRIS

Will Sell by Auction,

THIS EVENING (FRIDAY,)

At 6 o'Clock, on the premises, the whole of the

TIMBER

COMPRISED IN THE

Building of the Barn at The Homs, including a quantity of OAK.

The whole of the Timber to be cleared from off the premises within a fortnight of the day of Sale.

Ross, Friday, 9th May, 1862.   (DOBLES, PRINTER, ROSS,)

Poster advertising an auction of building material, Friday 9 May, 1862.

ABOVE: Lord Northfield, Chairman of the Development Commission, officially opened the Ashburton Industrial Estate, in March 1979. BELOW: The Industrial Estate has been built on the site of the railway station.

ABOVE: The imposing front of the present-day factory of Woodville Polymer Engineering Ltd. BELOW: Production at the Haigh Engineering factory.

ABOVE: Ross from Wilton Bridge, 1839. BELOW: A scene on the bridge with Redcoats escorting a prisoner, presumably from the gaol, now part of the White Lion Inn, Wilton. (From the painting by T. N. Webb, courtesy of Hereford City Museums)

Passage and Portway

Ross, well-placed on the fast roads network, is today familiar to the traveller between England and Wales, just as it was 400 years ago. The Act of 1597 for the building of Wilton Bridge described Ross as 'an ancient and great market town for all kinds of cattle, corn and other commodities (on) a great thoroughfare, passage or portway' from the counties of Hereford, Monmouth, Brecon, Carmarthen, Pembroke and most of South Wales to the City of London and other parts of England.

Wilton Bridge now carries the A40 road from London to Haverfordwest and all the attendant juggernauts of the late 20th century, but before it was built there were only stepping stones and ferry boats for the river crossing apart from one or two short-lived bridges. The 1597 Act said 'The passage boats there have been often so much overcharged with multitudes of people, that the same have sunk with the said people in the river, where thirty or forty of Her Majesty's subjects not long since have been drowned and utterly perished at once, and many others of them escaped by swimming, but very hardly with their lives..... Cattle and horses often have been drowned and spoiled to the great loss, terror, and imminent peril of such as have occasion to pass that way and to the great hindrance and impoverishment of the said town and of the county thereabouts'.

These were all good reasons for building the bridge and every town, parish, village and hamlet in the county, other than Hereford City, was required to find the money by tax or rate.

The river itself provided a channel for the passage of goods, but navigation was difficult, flooding in the winter and droughts in the summer being equal handicaps. In 1634, Colonel Sandys attempted to make the river navigable at all times by means of locks, but these were of little benefit and all were removed. Acts of Parliament in the reigns of Charles II and William III were intended to improve navigation, but nothing effectual was done.

Archdeacon William Coxe in his *Historical Tour through Monmouthshire* in 1801 noted that large quantities of coal were sent up river from Lydbrook in the Forest of Dean. In one day's travel down the river, he passed several barges towed by ten or eleven men who by great exertion drew the barges the 36 miles to Hereford in two days.

In 1808, Heath wrote: 'Most of the coal consumed in Hereford is brought up in barges. Various other articles, such as grocery, wines, spirituous liquor etc are conveyed at a much easier rate by land carriage'.

T. B. Watkins wrote in 1827, 'The barges at present employed on the river are from eighteen to thirty tons, and are towed by horses, a towing path having been formed under the powers of a recent Act. Great quantities of cider, hops, oak-bark, wool, wheat and timber are annually sent down to Brockweir, near Chepstow, where they are shipped off for London, Bristol, Ireland and other parts. With respect to the imports, if we except the articles of coal, slates, deals and heavy goods sold by shopkeepers, they are few and of little consequence'.

The wharf for the landing of coal and other goods was at Wilton, but the river traffic received a death blow with the coming of the railways.

Before this happened, Ross achieved a major position on the country's coaching routes, being about 18 hours from London. No fewer than 16 coaches were passing through the town on most days in the early 19th century. Every morning except Sunday, the *Rapid* called at 5.45 on its way from Hereford to London, and in the afternoons four coaches left for the capital: the Royal Mail from Milford, the *Champion* from Hereford, the *Paul Pry* from Brecon and the *Nimrod* from Carmarthen. Coaches were also providing a service in the opposite direction, and in addition, the *Rising Sun* called on its way from Hereford to Gloucester and the *Man of Ross* left at 8 am on Wednesday and Friday for Ledbury and Worcester.

On the morning of Friday, 14 September, 1821, the royal coach, carrying King George IV himself, arrived unexpectedly in Ross. The King had been visiting Ireland and because a violent storm had prevented the Royal Yacht from rounding the Lizard to sail to Portsmouth, he was compelled to land at Milford Haven and make the journey to London by road. He had suffered greatly from sea sickness, and had been on the road since early on Thursday with just a few hours' sleep at Brecon Priory, so he was probably not in the best of tempers when he reached Ross. The *Hereford Journal* correspondent reported briefly that the people were taken by surprise, otherwise 'many a loyal heart would have beaten high at the thought of showing their attachment to their Sovereign'.

But half a century later, a leading townsman, T. W. Purchas, gave a much more lucid description. He said of the King, 'He entered the town by the old Wilton Road and Dock Pitch (then the only way) and after a change of horses, and taking a glass of wine that was handed to him by Mrs Mary Howells, the landlady of the King's Head, much to the disappointment of the inhabitants, he drew down the blinds of the coach, intending to hurry on as quickly as possible. Greatly to his disgust, however, on arriving at the Nag's Head Inn, an unexpected obstacle barred his progress for a time. The carrier's waggon had arrived and, before unloading, the horses had been taken out. The place was so narrow that the King was obliged to wait while the horses were brought out again, and the waggon moved out of his way. The incident led to a great improvement of the town, as shortly afterwards, notice was sent from London that unless a better way was made through the town, the mail would be taken off the road, in consequence of which the present Gloucester Road was constructed'.

The Nag's Head, at the corner of High Street and Old Gloucester Road, was

116

converted into a shop some years ago and on the opposite side of the street is still to be seen 'King George's Rest' on a building which was also once a pub.

The carrier's waggon that incommoded the King was part of a service that operated at least twice a week between Ross and London, Bristol, Gloucester, Worcester, and North and South Wales.

The railways overwhelmed the coaches as much as they did the river traffic, but in 1890 the Comet four-horse coach was providing day outings to Abergavenny for 8s 6d and as late as 1906, C. A. Burroughs was running a daily coach between Ross and Raglan.

The Hereford, Ross and Gloucester Railway Company received its Act of Incorporation in 1851, and the next year Mr Peto contracted to build the line, which included four wayside stations besides Ross, four tunnels and three crossings of the Wye, for £230,000. The company was assisted by the Great Western Railway with a subscription of £25,000 towards its capital of £275,000. The GWR agreed to operate the line for 60 per cent of the gross receipts but in 1862 the local company was amalgamated with it.

The first trains ran into Ross amid great festivities on 1 June 1855, and in the first month, takings were £1,452 , a fraction under £16 per mile per week, which was considered very satisfactory. It was a single-track line, running for 21½ miles from Rotherwas to Grange Court and in 1869 made its mark in railway history books by becoming the first section of the Great Western Railway system to be converted from Brunel's broad gauge of 7ft to the standard gauge of 4ft 8½ ins.

In 1873, the Ross-Monmouth Railway Company opened the branch line down the Wye Valley, the trains being run by the GWR. Passenger services to Monmouth ended in 1959 and those on the Gloucester line in 1964. The next year saw the very last trains with the closing of the goods service to Lydbrook and Gloucester.

By then, the strategic position that Ross had enjoyed on the cross-country travel routes a century and a half before was being restored. When the Minister of Transport, Harold Watkinson, inaugurated the building of the M50 motorway (Ross Spur) in March, 1958, the only other motorway in the whole of Britain was the Preston by-pass. The 21 miles of motorway and two miles of Ross by-pass, built at a cost of £6 million, were opened in the autumn of 1960 and within the next decade the town became linked with motorways stretching to the Scottish border.

ABOVE: Wilton Bridge over the River Wye. CENTRE: In July, 1938, a lorry demolished the parapet as it crashed into the water. (Photo: R. E. Davies) RIGHT: The sun dial that Jonathan Barrow built on Wilton Bridge in 1718.BELOW:The building of Bridstow Bridge, to carry the Ross by-pass, in 1960. The bridge has three spans and a total length of 353 ft.

118

ABOVE: In times of flood a more apt name for the town would be 'Ross-on-Sea'. BELOW: The Wye in flood on Sunday 18 December, 1910. This was the highest recorded level since 1852.

LEFT ABO
brook in
Meadows in
BELOW: W
at Wilton Bri
of 1963. C
Brookend S
ghostly moo
John Hall
when the v
century v

120

e Rudhall
er Broad
ber, 1929.
oss the river
great freeze
Floods in
IGHT: A
taken by
rch, 1947,
ds of the
ir peak.

ROSS TURNPIKE
TOLLS
TO BE LET.

Notice is hereby Given,

That a meeting of the Trustees of the ROSS TURNPIKE ROADS, will be holden at the house of JAMES BARRETT, at the ROYAL HOTEL, in ROSS, on WEDNESDAY, the 15th day of MAY next, at Twelve of the clock at noon ; at which meeting the Tolls arising at the several Toll Gates, upon the Ross Turnpike Roads, in the county of Hereford, called or known by the names of WILTON, PENCRAIG, MARSH, HOWNHALL, RYEFORD, CORPS-CROSS, COUGHTON, WALFORD, OVER-ROSS, GATSFORD, COLDBROUGH, and MARCLE GATES, with the STOP-GATES thereto belonging, will be put up to be Let by Auction or otherwise, to the highest bidder, for one or more Years, to commence at Twelve of the clock at noon, on the 15th or such other day of May next, as the Trustees shall appoint, in one Lot, or in such other Lots, and under such conditions, regulations, provisions, and restrictions, and in such manner, as may then be determined upon by the Trustees, pursuant to Acts passed in the third and fourth Years of the reign of King George the Fourth, " for regulating Turnpike Roads." And whoever happens to be the highest bidder or bidders, for such Lot or Lots respectively, must forthwith pay one Month's rent in advance, at which the Tolls may be let, and give security, with sufficient sureties, to the satisfaction of the Trustees of the said roads, for payment of the residue of the rent, by equal Monthly payments in advance, to the said Trustees, or their Treasurer, for the time being, and for the observance of the conditions of Letting.

WILLIAM GARDNER,
Clerk to the Trustees.

Every bidder will be required to make a deposit of ONE HUNDRED POUNDS upon his first bidding, which will be returned, except to the highest bidder, who will be required immediately after the Auction, to pay one Month's rent in advance, and if he does not comply with the conditions of Letting, the said One Hundred Pounds will be forfeited to the Trust.

Ross, April 15th, 1839.

PRINTED BY W. FARROR, STAMP OFFICE, ROSS.

The turnpike tolls were offered for sale in 1839.

LEFT: A watercolour by Cecilia Armitage of the turnpike gate at Wilton, removed on 31 December, 1872. RIGHT: Gloucester Road before it was on the A40 trunk road from London to Fishguard. BELOW: Dock Pitch, now Wye Street, was the only way into Ross from the river until Wilton Road was built. In February 1831 a man was drowned during flooding and in 1833 a new road was made.

ABOVE: Wye Street in the early 20th century. BELOW: Red Hill, showing
the two roads leading out of the town.

ABOVE: Looking down Broad Street in the days of the horse-drawn vehicle, and BELOW: looking up the same street in 1935, when the car was still unobtrusive.

ABOVE: High Street before the traffic came. CENTRE: In the great blizzard of March, 1947, snow blocked High Street. LEFT: Robey Steam Wagon No 5, used by S. Llewellyn and Son, coal merchants and transport contractors. RIGHT: A novel form of transport, seen outside the old Ross Council Schools.

ABOVE: High Street choked with traffic, and BELOW: as it was in the early
1950s.

ABOVE: Early Brush car, pictured in the Station Approach about 1901-02.
The owner, C. L. Llewellyn, is seen with his son, his wife, and his sister.
CENTRE: Early steam engines. BELOW: The railway station as it was
before passenger services were withdrawn in 1964.

128

DOWN TRAINS.

STATIONS.	WEEK DAYS.						SUN-DAYS.
	1, 2, 3.	1, 2, 3.	Ex. 1 & 2.	1, 2, 3.	1 & 2.	Ex. 1 & 2.	1, 2, 3.
	A.M.	A.M.	A.M.	A.M.	A.M.	P.M.	A.M.
PADDINGTON *Dp*	..	6 0	9 45	7 15	10 40	4 50	8 0
Reading ...... "	..	7 15	10 30	9 5	11 40	5 40	9 40
Oxford........ "	..	7 25	9 28	9 15	..	5 30	..
Bristol........ "	6 35	9 0	11 20	1 25	1 25	6 50	10 0
Weymouth .... "	..	6 10	..	9 0	..	..	..
Swindon ...... "	..	9 20	11 45	1 30	1 30	6 52	1 5
Cirencester .... "	..	9 40	11 50	1 35	1 35	7 0	..
Stroud .... "	..	10 30	12 40	2 40	2 40	7 45	2 15
Cheltenham .... "	8 0	10 30	12 45	3 0	3 0	8 0	2 30
GLOUCESTER *Ar*	8 20	11 0	1 5	3 15	3 15	8 10	2 50

	A.M.	A.M.	P.M.	P.M.		P.M.	P.M.
GLO'STER ...*Dep.*	8 25	11 10	1 10	3 20		8 20	3 0
Grange Court .. "	8 45	11 35	1 30	3 50		8 45	3 25
Longhope...... "	8 55	11 50	.	4 0		8 55	3 40
Mitcheldean Rd. "	9 5	12 0	..	4 10		9 5	3 50
ROSS .... "	9 15	12 10	1 55	4 25		9 15	4 5
Fawley .... "	9 25	12 20	..	4 35		9 25	4 17
Holme Lacy.... "	9 35	12 30	..	4 45		9 35	4 27
HEREFORD *Ar* "	9 45	12 45	2 25	5 0		9 45	4 40

These Times are inserted for Public convenience, but their correctness is not guaranteed.

HEREFORD *Dep.*	9 50		2 40	5 15	..	8 20
Leominster ....*Arr.*	10 20		3 15	5 50	..	8 47
Kington ...... "	11 10		4 20	7 35	..	..
Ludlow ...... "	10 40		3 42	6 14	..	9 5
Shrewsbury .... "	11 45		4 55	7 25	..	10 0

ABOVE: Advertising leaflet of 1860, showing the timetable of the Hereford, Ross and Gloucester Railway. BELOW: After lying derelict for ten years, the railway station was finally demolished in 1975.

129

ABOVE: In July 1912 great excitement was caused when the first aeroplane in Ross touched down on the golf course at the foot of Penyard Hill. The French pilot M. Salmet, is pictured with golf club. CENTRE: The scene at Wilton in the days of commercial traffic on the river; engraving by D. Cox from W. Radclyffe's painting. BELOW: This aircraft hangar in Butcher's motor engineering works was used early this century by William Butcher and his son-in-law Ernest Barkes, who built an aircraft of 'wood and canvas'. INSET:Apart from The Man of Ross House, the only remaining timber-framed house in the streets is this one in the High Street. The former Saracen's Head, it is now an auctioneer's offices.

130

The Wye Discovered

The Reverend John Egerton never knew the impact he made on the future. He could not know that the boat excursions he arranged were the opening moves of a venture that in a little over two centuries would annually be pouring a million pounds into the economy of Ross, would create an entirely new industry and would even lead to the name of the town being adjusted to 'Ross-on-Wye'.

John Egerton was a wealthy man, grandson of the Earl of Bridgewater, son of Henry Egerton, Bishop of Hereford, who in 1745 made him Rector of Ross. John stayed for 26 years before moving on to become successively Bishop of Bangor, of Lichfield, and of Durham, but however great was the influence of his pastoral care, it is unlikely that it was as far reaching as that which he exercised on the Wye Valley.

As a unique and satisfying diversion for the noble relatives and wealthy friends he invited to stay at the Rectory, he had a pleasure boat built so that they could be towed to Monmouth and Chepstow. They were astounded by a beauty that had stayed hidden for so long. A few miles from Ross the fertile fields are replaced by hills clothed with woodland dropping to the water's edge. The solid ruins of the castle at Goodrich, the white craggy Seven Sisters rocks towering above the Symonds Yat gorge: mile after mile the grandeur was breathtaking.

In the drawing rooms of Britain they were talking about the discovery made within their own kingdom. Prime Minister Lord North relaxed from his dealings with the troublesome American colonists by bringing his family to Ross for the Wye Tour. The poet, Thomas Gray, was spellbound by what he saw. 'Its banks are a succession of nameless beauties', he wrote a few weeks before his death in 1771.

Another parson, the Rev William Gilpin, of Hampshire, widened the river's fame. In his *Observations on the River Wye* in 1770, he wrote, 'The Wye flows in a gentle uninterrupted stream and adorns through its various reaches a succession of the most picturesque scenes. The beauty of these scenes arises chiefly from two cirumstances, the lofty banks of the river and its mazy course'.

It was not the most enticing language, but soon those who had the means were following the fashion and coming to Ross. They went down the river in boats lightly constructed, used with or without a sail and navigated by three men. By 1827 as many as eight boats a day were leaving Ross, and Heath remarked, 'The proprietor of the vessel accompanies them (the tourists) so that the ear is not pained with a coarseness of language too frequently heard from the navigators of public rivers'.

The cost of travelling the 21 river miles to Monmouth was a guinea and a half, and of the two-day journey to Chepstow, three guineas, plus provisions for the boatmen.

The Royal Hotel was built in 1837 and the old Swan Hotel was rebuilt in 1867 to accommodate the visitors, and even the new and exciting form of travel provided by the railway did not diminish the popularity of the river. In 1859, Joseph Evans, of the Post Office, was advertising daily excursions, except Sundays, to Goodrich for one shilling, to Monmouth for five shillings and to Chepstow for ten shillings.

Royalty went by boat from Ross to Symonds Yat in 1891. The future Queen Mary, 24-year-old Princess Victoria Mary of Teck, with her parents, the Duke and Duchess of Teck and her brother, Prince Alexander George, arrived in a carriage drawn by four greys which was escorted through the festive town by the Shropshire Yeomanry and Ross Brass Band. At the Dock, the royal party and their companions embarked in three boats, manned by watermen wearing scarlet jerseys, white flannel trousers and white straw hats with scarlet bands.

The party disembarked at Goodrich to take lunch at the court with Mr and Mrs H. C. Moffat, and afterwards continued to Symonds Yat where 16 decorated boats formed an aquatic guard of honour. The visitors disembarked at Washings Ferry and came back to Ross in a four-horse drag and three carriages.

At the start of the new century, in May 1902, the Ross boatbuilding family of Henry Dowell and Son launched the stern wheel steamship *The Wilton Castle,* with a capacity for 100 passengers and a speed of eight miles an hour. For over two decades it plied the river, probably the biggest craft seen on the Wye, being 65ft long with a 10ft beam.

In the 1920s Dowell's were running day trips in rowing boats for parties of four or more down to Monmouth at a cost of eight shillings a passenger. They would leave Ross at 10.30 am, pause an hour at Goodrich for a visit to the castle and have lunch at Lydbrook. Approaching Symonds Yat, the passengers might leave the boat and walk three-quarters of a mile over the hill to rejoin it, or stay in it as it went round the four and a half mile loop. Monmouth would be reached at about 5 pm.

Since the Second World War, craft on the river at Ross have been limited to those of the Rowing Club or canoes, the salmon and coarse fishermen being united in their opposition to any large pleasure boats.

The town has long been conscious of the value of attracting tourists and in the last century the names 'Gateway of the Wye' and 'Ross-on-Wye' began to come into the local vocabulary. The former irritated those in neighbouring towns who would not accept the justification of the claim, and the latter annoyed many of the older residents, who even after the Post Office gave official recognition to 'Ross-on-Wye' in 1931 stubbornly contined to give their address as 'Ross, Herefordshire'.

The first corporate body to state as an objective the promotion of Ross as an inland resort was the Traders' Association, which came into being in 1909 and published a guide book the following year. The association changed its name to the Ross Improvement and Publicity Association in 1922 and to the Chamber of Commerce in 1930, and guide books were published until 1970.

Also promoting the town are the Ross Hoteliers and Caterers Association, founded in 1948 and the Wyedean Tourist Board, inaugurated in 1946 and now under the aegis of the Heart of England Tourist Board, a regional board set up by the English Tourist Board in accordance with the Development of Tourism Act, 1969. The tourist of today rarely has the opportunity of travelling by water, but whether on footpath or on tarmac road he still finds a valley wrapped in tranquility and beauty.

ABOVE: The tour of the Wye, advertised in the *Ross and Archenfield Gazette* on 9 June, 1855. BELOW: The mid-19th century engraver made a composite scene of the sailing boats, barges and rowing boats on the horseshoe bend.

ABOVE: A view of Ross from a slope at Benhall Farm. BELOW: A 19th century impression of the town from the horseshoe bend.

THE
ROSS GUIDE;

CONTAINING

An Historical and Topographical

ACCOUNT OF THE TOWN;

A DESCRIPTION OF ITS

PUBLIC BUILDINGS,

CHURCH, DISSENTING MEETING-HOUSES,

its

Schools, Trade, Commerce, Navigation,

AND OTHER

Interesting Particulars relating to the Place.

TO WHICH IS PREFIXED A

BRIEF MEMOIR OF J. KYRLE, Esq.

COMMONLY CALLED THE MAN OF ROSS.

Also a Description of

THE PRINCIPAL SEATS,

AND

REMARKABLE PLACES IN THE NEIGHBOURHOOD.

Together with a particular Account of the

POSTS, STAGE COACHES, WAGGONS &c.

———

Hereford:

PRINTED AND SOLD BY T. B. WATKINS.

———

1827.

LEFT: *The Ross Guide* of 1827. RIGHT: Lloyd George, seen leaving the Royal Hotel, often stopped at Ross en route from North Wales to London. BELOW: Coracles survived on the Wye until 1910. This scene on the horseshoe bend more than 100 years ago, shows on the bank Sammy Jones, who died in 1882, aged 93.

LEFT ABOVE: James Woolf put up this arch across Gloucester Road when the Herefordshire Agricultural Society held its show at the Camp Meadow in June 1887. The photo was taken a week later on Queen Victoria's Golden Jubilee Day. Queen Victoria's Diamond Jubilee in 1897: CENTRE: A fine display at James Price's glazier's shop, 9 Broad Street, and BELOW: the Market Place bedecked. CENTRE ABOVE: B. Powle drew Ross from the Wye before the Royal Hotel was built in 1837. (Courtesy Hereford City Museums). BELOW: A page of adverts from *Lascelles Directory of Herefordshire*, 1851. RIGHT ABOVE: On 26 September, 1891, 'B' Company

SARAH NEW

HOPE & ANCI

NEAR THE RIV

BASKET & SIEV

PLEASURE BOAT PI

Boats for Excursions on the Wye

Abbey, and Chep

BOATS OF EVERY DESCRIPTION C

of the 1st Herefordshire Rifle Volunteers for riverside when the Duke and Duchess of daughter Princess Victoria Mary (later Qu Symonds Yat. CENTRE: John Rowberry, C reads the Proclamation of Queen Elizabeth February, 1952. BELOW: On 24 April, 195 Edinburgh visited Ross and received the acc Market Place and Broad Street. (

ard of honour at the
Prince George and
y) went by boat to
f the Urban Council,
e Market House in
een and the Duke of
ousands packing the
L. Ward)

Hot air balloonist Ian Ashpole took this photo as he drifted over Ross on Carnival Day, 1979. (Photo: Ian Ashpole/*Ross-on-Wye Advertiser*)

Diary of Ross-on-Wye
1086-1979

1086	Mention of Ross in Domesday Book
c1138	King Stephen grants Robert de Bethune a Thursday market
1241	King Henry III grants three day fairs
1277	First recorded Rector, William de Ablaniat
1305	Two burgesses attend Parliament
1316	Dedication of altars in St Mary's Parish Church
1559	Bishops' rule ends as Crown takes possession of manors
1575	William Rudhall rebuilds almshouses in Church Street
1597	Act of Parliament for building Wilton Bridge
1637	Plague decimates Ross. Birth of John Kyrle
1645	Scots army on rampage. King Charles I pauses in Ross on way to Hereford
1662	Opening of Independent Church
c1670	Building of Market House
1676	Friends Meeting House built at Brookend
1709	Blue Coat School founded
1749	John and Charles Wesley visit
1770	William Gilpin's praise of river makes Wye tour fashionable
1786	Walter Scott's will saves Bluecoat School which is given his name. Birth of James Cowles Prichard
1788	Building of workhouse which later developed into Dean Hill Hospital
1818	Kingsmill Evans buys manors of Ross and Ross Foreign
1819	First Baptist Church built at Ross
1821	King George IV passes through town
1830	Act for Improving Ross leads to local government by Commissioners
1837	British and Foreign School opened
1837	Royal Hotel built
1852	Death of a maid in New Street fire awakens the town to the need for efficient fire engine
1855	Hereford-Ross-Gloucester railway opened
1859	Observatory founded
1862	Corn Exchange built
1865	Second Ross Improvement Act
1866	Gospel Hall moved to present site in Henry Street
1867	*Ross Gazette* established
1868	Congregational Church opened
1869	Prospect riots
1871	Cattle market provided
1872	Turnpikes abolished
1873	Ross-Monmouth railway line opened
1874	Council schools in Cantilupe Road opened
1879	Cottage Hospital built
1881	New Baptist Church built
1887	Alton Court water works and reservoir built
1891	Duke and Duchess of Teck and Princess Victoria (afterwards Queen Mary) went by boat from Ross to Symonds Yat
1895	Urban Council came into being
1896	Severe earth tremors
1899	Post Office in Gloucester Road built
1902	Ross Electric Light and Power Company came into operation
1906	Fire station built on site of old parish pound
1912	Grammar School opened
1928	Walter Scott School closed
1931	Official name changed to 'Ross-on-Wye'. Church of St Frances of Rome built
1934	St Joseph's Convent established
1939	New Theatre and Corn Exchange destroyed by fire
1944	Cemetery at Tudorville dedicated
1952	Urban Council puts £50 prize in salvage competition towards costs of acquiring coat of arms and chairman's chain of office
1953	Secondary Modern School opened
1956	Brewing of beer ended at Ross. Opening of Haigh Engineering Company's factory
1957	Queen and Duke of Edinburgh visit Ross
1958	New police station opened. Formation of Sports Centre Association
1959	Closing of Ross-Monmouth railway line
1960	By-pass opened in September and M50 motorway in November. Ross Water Undertaking absorbed into Herefordshire Water Board. Building of 11 shops at George Place
1961	Woodville Rubber Company starts production at Ross
1964	Closing of Hereford-Ross-Gloucester railway passenger service
1968	School buildings at Cantilupe Road condemned
1969	Building of new fire station at Hildersley
1970	Ashfield Park Primary School opened
1973	Swimming pool opened
1974	Urban Council superseded by South Herefordshire District Council. Town Council formed and Ross has a Mayor again
1975	Observatory closed
1978	Ross twins with Norman town of Condé-Sur-Noireau
1979	Comprehensive education introduced, John Kyrle High School being formed out of the Grammar School and Overross School

Bibliography

Anthony, Edward, *Herefordshire Cricket,* Anthony Bros, 1903
Beattie, E. H., *The Parish Church of St Mary the Virgin, Ross*
Burke's Peerage, 1967
Coxe, William, *Historical Tour through Monmouthshire,* 1801
Curnock, N., *Wesleys's Journal,* 1909
Dew, E. N., *Extracts from Cathedral Registers,* 1275-1535, 1932
Duncumb, J., *History and Antiquities of the County of Hereford,* 1804
Encyclopaedia Britannica, 1953
Fosbroke, T. D., *The Wye Tour,* 1822
Gilpin, William, *Observations on the River Wye,* 1770
Heath, Charles, *Excursion Down the Wye,* 1808
Hutton, E.A., *A Book of the Wye,* Methuen, 1911
Moir, A. L., *Bishops of Hereford,* 1964
Moir, Esther, *The Discovery of Britain,* Routledge and Kegan Paul, 1964
Morris, M. H., *Reflections of Ross-on-Wye, 1973*
Page, W., *Victoria History of the County of Hereford,* Constable, 1908
Pearce, K. W., and Rev G. R. O'Neill,*Centenary of Ross Methodist Church,* 1967
Reade, Compton, *Memorials of Old Herefordshire,* Bemrose, 1904
Robinson, C. J., *Mansions and Manors of Herefordshire,* 1872
Sharpe, C. J., *The Church Bells of Herefordshire,* 1972
Smith, L. Tolumin, *Leland's Itinerary in England,* Bell, 1906
Towers, L. T. A., *History of the Congregational Church meeting at Ross-on-Wye,* 1962
Trevor, J. C., *Prichard's Life and Works,* Man, 1948
Tupper, F and Bladen Ogle, *Map's de Nugis Curialium,* 1924
Watkins, Alfred, *The Old Standing Crosses of Herefordshire,* 1930
Watkins, T. B., *The Ross Guide,* 1827
Webb, John, *Civil War in Herefordshire,* Longmans, 1879
Whiting, Edith Southall, *Story of the Quakers in Ross,* MS unpublished
Woolhope Naturalists' Field Club Transactions, 1851-74
Encyclopaedia Britannica
Directories: *Burrows Wye Valley,* 1905: Jakeman and Carver, *Herefordshire,* 1890: *Kelly's, Herefordshire,* 1870:
Lascelles and Co, *Herefordshire,* 1851: *Pigot, J and Co,* 1830, 1835: Powle, R. *Handbook to Ross and Archenfield,* 1863
Newspapers: *Ross Gazette: Man of Ross: Ross and Archenfield Gazette: Hereford Times: Hereford Journal.*

Index

Subscribers
Presentation Copies

1   Ross-on-Wye Town Council
2   South Herefordshire District Council
3   Hereford and Worcs County Council
4   Ross-on-Wye Library
5   Hereford Library
6   Leominster Library
7   Ledbury Library
8   Dame Margaret Shepherd DBE

9 Martin H. Morris	55 E. W. Evans	160 Peggyanne Stevenson	203 Group Capt J. B. Lewis RAF (Retd)
10 Clive & Carolyn Birch	56 Anne Riches	161 A. J. Evans	204 Derek T. Preece
11 Josephine Lane	57 Mrs J. Smith	162 Kenneth Higton	205
12 Jane Minton	58 Miss C. Abell	163 D. A. Colburn	206 Mrs E. Walker
13 Helen Morris	59 Brigadier A.F.L. Clive	164 W. J. & G. R. Marfell	207 Clive Brooks
14 Emma Marie Lane	60 Keith Shawcross	165 Miss B.Z.M. Robbins	208 Paul Hudson
15 Miss C. Morris	61 Mrs Ruby Griffin	166 D. I. Criddle	209 John W. Pugh JP
16 Mrs N. W. Jackson	62 Mervyn James Ltd	167 Mr & Mrs M. A. Alldred	210 G. A. Rogers
17 Miss G. A. Morris	63 J. C. Coombes	168 D. Y. Watson	211 J. S. Reece
18 Mrs Margaret E. Powell	64 J. & E. Dobbins	169 M. A. T. Ashton	212 W. F. Hodson
19 Miss Mary Morris	65 Manley Power	170 Martyn Smith	213 J.M. Brandram Jones
20 Arthur A. Morris	66 Edward C. Allen	171 D. Webb	214
21 Mrs Josephine Hogg	67 Mrs J. Freeman	172 Miss Trafford	215 Roy Wade
22 E. Rowley Morris JP MA	68 R. Okell	173 S. E. Prosser	216 Mrs V. E. Walters
23 Mrs S. W. Kelly	69 Mrs M. Lewis	174 Harvey's	217 Mervyn Tommey JP
24 Ernest Morris	70 Mrs Charles Truelove	175 Mr & Mrs G. Davis	218 G. D. T. Prime
25 Rodney Sandell	71 D. A. Lewis	176 Trevor Collier	219 R. E. Gibbons
26 Stephen C. Stoner	72 Mrs K. E. Macready	177 W. G. Watkins	220 Raymond G. V. Thomas
27 Thomas W. Passey JP	73 Dr B. S. Smith	178 O. R. & J. R. Colcombe	221 D. C. Davies MPS
28 Donald Grigg	74	179 W. A. C. Netting	222 Colin Lewis
29 Mrs E. Farrington	75 Air Cdr S. W. Lane CBE	180 Wyedean Tourist Board	223 M. J. A. Winch
30 Mrs Barbara Garner	76 John A. Constance	181 Mrs J. M. Jones	224 William Rowley Morris
31 Mrs E. M. Luker	77 Robert Murray	182 Paul Rynehart	225 P. J. Smith
32 Prebendary John Thursfield	78 A. G. R. Cross	183	226 F. E. Clarke
33 Arthur Stonadge	79 Mrs J. Copping	184 Mr & Mrs D. B. East	227 John Horner
34 Mrs E. G. Butcher	80 C. G. Hall	185 Ivor Jones	228 Sandra Oakley
35 Miss M. A. Butcher	81 Mrs P. M. Wilkinson	186 Andrew John Middlecote	229 Margaret Haine
36 Peter Chard	82 A. C. Netting	187 Caroline Hession	230 C. Holden
37 G. P. Morris	83 G. Painter	188 Mrs D. Bennett	231 D. Hudson
38 R. G. Hicks	84 Richard Lee	189 Dr A. Rogers	232 Rev A. N. Graham
39 Nigel Heins	85 R. Thomas	190 Bridget Like	233 R. H. Clayfield
40 Peggy Tonge	86 A. F. Dobbyn	191 David Massey	234 Mrs I. L. Davies
41 R. D. G. Morse	87 Mrs W. Taylor	192 Mr & Mrs T. H. Pickles	235 R. R. W. Barnett
42 Stephen M. Shutt	88 Stan Witts	193 N. C. Bricknell	236
43 J. F. Ashby	89 Ian Davenport	194	237 Mrs Anne Taylor
44 E. J. Rowberry	90 Alfred Jennings	195 Mrs E. M. Rees	238 T. G. Williams
45 Lt Col I.G. Mathews	91 Robert C. Pearson	196 Mr & Mrs C. Dennis Footitt	239 G. B. Williams
46 Kenneth Riches	92 B. J. Auty	197 James Edward Farmer	240 John H. Lythgoe
47 R. G. Williams	93 B. C. Hackett OBE	198 Mrs E. M. Farmer	241 Geoffrey Benjamin Lancashire
48 Mrs Ann Morris	94 JP	199 Mr & Mrs S. R. Ellis	242 Edna May Lancashire
49 John Martin	95 D. F. Nelson	200 Leslie Price	243 Jane Bailes
50 Maureen Morris	96 Paul Eward	201 R.L. Price MA, MSc	244 Noele Gordon
51 Mrs G. Rowlands	97 F. R. Pugh	202 R. H. Roff	245 Lloyd A. Stevens
52 Mr & Mrs D. J. Anderson	98 G. Gwatkin		246 Wolf Tools Ltd
53 Mr & Mrs Alan Brown	99 C. L. Burrows		247
54 Ian Walker	100 Keith Tofield JP		248 G. W. Bunting
	109		
	110 Woodville Polymer		
	159 Engineering Ltd		

143

249	R. J. Bevan	311	Janet Bagnall
250	Martin Morris	312	Cdr E. J. Prevost
251 259	Miss C. Morris	313	Ivan Dazeley
260	Miss C. E. Cole	314	E. J. Evans
261	M. A. Boaden	315	W. T. Davies
262	R. Highley	316	Gwyneth Young
263	N. G. McCready	317	John Hall
264	Mrs M. H. Clatworthy	318	J. K. Gabb
265	Miss G. A. Wise	319	C. H. Wright
266	B. S. Webb	320	Brian T. Richards
267	Miss J. E. Ireland	321	Raymond Scruton-Evans
268	Mrs M. Brook	322	Richard Winnel
269	E. J. Godwin	323	Joe & Mary Winnel
270	A. Morris	324	Mr & Mrs Dennis Minton
271 272	C. E. Attfield	325	Gary Minton
273	Miss Penelope E. Morgan	326	R. M. Humphreys
274	Richard Rudall	327	B. C. Hackett OBE
275	S. G. Little	328	J. H. Edwards
276	F. G. Scudamore	329	E. N. Preece
277	R. P. Morgan	330	Mrs S. J. Griffin
278	A. J. P. Greer	331	C. J. Metcalfe
279	Mrs R. Owen	332	G. Haunton
280	Dr & Mrs Alan Clark	333	Frederick Howard Passey
281	Mr & Mrs Albert Clark	334	Les Marshall
282	Chris Arnold	335	Mrs M. Edwards
283	J. E. Powell	336	Mr & Mrs L. Skelton
284	John E. Trivett	337	Marjorie Vera Parry
285	John Kyrle High School	338	David Matthews
286		339	Dame Margaret Shepherd
287	Clive Joyce	343	
288	Mr & Mrs J. M. Acheson	344 345	D. F. J. Walker
289	John David Weeds	346	H. E. Godfrey
290	L.J. Harris	347	Mrs P. E. Norris
291	Andrew Sime	348	Mrs E. Shinton
292	E. Capstick	349	J. H. Griswold
293	G. M. Hughes	350	Arthur J. Hughes
294	R. G. Purvis	351	Mrs P. M. Birchley
295	Mrs A. G. Williams	352	P. P. Thomas
296	Dr G. Marner Lloyd	353	Arthur Griffiths
297	J. L. Wallin	354	D. M. Smith
298	Frank Knight	355	S. Paul Johnson
299	Stephen C. Daniels	356 357	Mrs D. Kersley
300 301	R. H. Gadd	358	Dr Gerhard Hermann
302	Paul Scudamore	359	C. N. Whitehouse
303	William T. Davies	360	I.G. & M. Bennett
304	William Chinn	361	H.K. Prisk
305	T. R. Blenkin	362	Ross Laundry Co Ltd
306	Mr & Mrs P. Plumley	363	L. D. Harrold
307	E. R. Arnold	364	G. E. Jenkins
308	Mrs Joyce Thomas	365	Jon & Heather Hurley
309	Paul Deneen	366	Monmouth District Council
310	A. J. Rhymes	367	Mrs M. Reeve-Tucker

368	Mrs E. Webb	421	M. H. V. Littlefield
369	Colin Shepherd MP	422	John Kyrle High School
370	Mrs K. M. Davis	423	Miss Mildred Betty
371	Francis Moran	424	Joe Hillaby
372	G. E. Morgan	425	Barry R. Butler
373	R. W. Andrews	426	T. R. Steward
374	Mr & Mrs Ray Thomas	427	Dr J. C. Nicholson
375	Mrs T. R. Sainsbury	428	R. A. Jones
376		429	F. Whitty
377	Alice V. Caterer	430	Judith & William Hazelton
378	E. T. Rawlins	431	N. S. L. Llewellyn
379	Leonard William Webb	432	D. C. Moore
380	John J. Roberts	433	Mrs H. Warren
381 382	Sisters of St Joseph	434	L. E. Boll
383	Mrs E. M. Porter MBE	435	W. Chinn
384	G.K. & M. Peckham	436	W. J. Chinn
385	Mrs I. M. Bromhead	437	Dennis Butcher
386	Mrs E. Norman	438	Janette Symonds
387	H. P. Pullen	439	Rev J. F. Bowen
388	P. M. James	440	Richard Houghton
389	Mrs Matthews	441	Malcolm Jenkins
390	Mrs G. K. Harper	442	Mary Eunice Roberts
391	Mrs D. M. Bevan	443	Gordon Keay
392	Mrs E. Langley	444	Susan Bulgin
393	Dr C. R. Hartshorn	445	Peter F. Wyndham Pember
394	Mrs E. Williams	446	F. J. Handley
395	T. Wigney	447	F. E. Okell
396	Miss M. Smith	448	C. L. Doughty
397	Mrs Brenda Ruck	449	Mrs K. E. Innes
398	F. W. W. Roche	450	C. F. Morris
399	B. C. Jenkins	451	E. J. McCormick
400	Francis Green	452	Mr & Mrs N. J. Nelson
401	R. M. T. Watson	453	D. E. Gwyer
402	J. C. Taylor	454	Ray & Carolyn Hill
403	S. W. Reeves	455	Heather A. Cocker
404	David Read	456	Mrs K. W. Pearce
405	Malcolm Read	457	Mr & Mrs R. Sharp
406	Victoria and Albert Museum	458	Miss M. Haverson
407	Philip N. Dazeley	459	Mrs J. A. Watts
408	Hereford Educational Development Centre	460	Mrs Elsie Broadhead
409	G. J. Hurst	461	Kenneth Riches
410	Gordan Lucas	462	Chriss Ollis
411	Margaret Lucas	463	Alec D. Baines
412	Jeff McKenzie	464	P. R. Handley
413	R. S. Vivian	465	Miss Vera Childs
414 415	Andrew Jackson	466 467	W. J. Parkman MBE
416	Mrs F. M. Holland Davies	468	Mrs T. Marshall
417	Mrs S. Whittal-Williams	469	The Headmistress, St Joseph's RC School
418	P. Jamison	470	Woodville Polymer
419	M. G. Davy	489	Engineering Ltd
420	R. J. Childs		

Remaining names unlisted

ENDPAPERS: FRONT—Engraving made from a watercolour by J. A. Sanders of Bath in 1810. BACK—Plan of Ross by Thomas Wakeman, 1823.

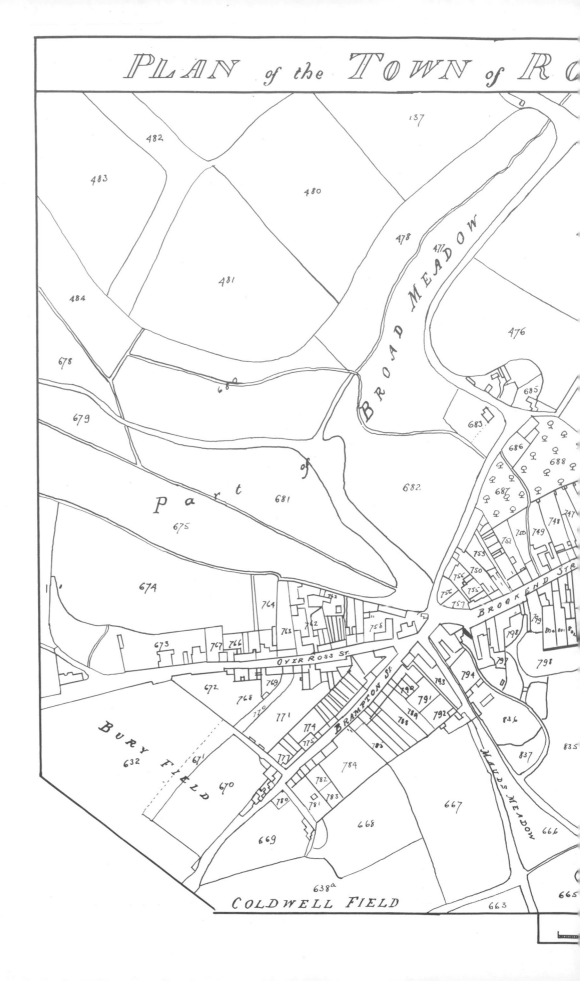

137

482

483

480

481

478

BROAD MEADOW

477

476

484

685

678

686

688

680

683

679

687

682

681

748 747

of

749

675

Part

750

752

674

751

753

750

756

755

757

764

762

799

800 801 80

761

782

758

BROOKEND STR

673

767 766

769

OVER ROSS ST.

798

793 794

672

768

BRAMPTON ST.

796

791

836

770

771

792

790

789

797

798

774

784

835

773

775

BURY FIELD

632

671

782

783

837

667

670

780

781

666

669

668

MEUDS MEADOW

638ᵃ

665

COLDWELL FIELD

663